MANLY FOOD

MANLY FOOD

SIMON CAVE

QUADRILLE

CONTENTS

INTRODUCTION

What is Manly Food? You already know instinctively. Answer these multiple choice questions if you don't believe me.

A Manly steak is:
(a) A medallion of beef fillet on a bed of subtle cream tarragon emulsion.
(b) A burned and bloody side of cow.

A Manly dessert is:
(a) A cupcake.
(b) A hunk of cheese.

A Manly cocktail is:
(a) Fruit and cream-based with lots of different colors and an umbrella.
(b) Tastes mostly of alcohol, and is bitter, sour, or salty, or a combination of all three.

B, right? Of course. If you answered (a) cupcake, you were not taking this seriously and shame on you! This book is all about full-on food: the meaty, hearty, bold, adventurous, and downright greedy side of food. It is about no-holds-barred, all-guns-blazing, all-action cooking. Sounds fun, doesn't it? Want to explore your Manly side? Saddle up, pilgrim.

THE RULES

The first rule of manly food is Flavor First.
The second rule of manly food is *Flavor First*.
The third rule of manly food is Cook with Attitude.
The fourth rule of manly food is Respect your Tools.

1. & 2. FLAVOR FIRST

It is often said that men only like to eat meat, and that we order steak in a restaurant predictably, every single time. But that is missing the point. Meat is just a reliable shortcut to flavor. And flavor is what we want—all we want. Life is just too short for genteel, and merely nice. The other guy or gal can have that. I'll take the "My God, that's amazing, did I order that? Yesss."

Manly Food is all about big, bold flavors that are still fighting as you ingest them. It's about taking a stand against the modern tyranny of bland. Let's hear it for honest flavors and straight-talking discourse about food. You are a grown-up, so decide for yourself how to be healthy; but as adults, we're not going to pretend that salt and fat don't make things taste really good. They do. Similarly, if a dish calls for a lot of chili, garlic, or funky fish sauce—if that's what it's meant to taste of—then that's what you will find here. None of the recipes have been toned down, filtered, softened, or homogenized. We are in the business of exploring, so alongside old favorites, you'll find plenty of unusual flavors and ingredients, too. While it's well worth tracking down some of the exotic ingredients, cooking ought to be an exploration. No-one should get too worried about adhering strictly to the recipe. Trust your own judgment, and above all, have a playful approach to balancing flavors and ingredients.

Having said that, get real about ingredients. Not all ingredients are created equal. A free-range chicken tastes better than a battery one. Well-hung, matured beef tastes better than the mushy mass served up as steak in many grocery stores. Wild salmon tastes better than farmed. A bad wine is still bad when you add it to a stew. If you don't search out good-quality ingredients, your food will never be as good as it could have been.

Be true to the dish. Some dishes are fast by nature, and if you need something quick, these are obviously the dishes for you. Other dishes take an age (not of your time, usually—you just need to leave them in the refrigerator or at a simmer, and stir them once in a while). And that is as it should be; they are meant to be like this. The Manly Way is to respect this, not cheat or cut corners. If a job is worth doing, it is worth doing well.

3. COOK WITH ATTITUDE

'Tis an ill cook that cannot lick his own fingers.
—Shakespeare, *Romeo and Juliet* IV.ii

Cook without fear. If you are in the wilderness and stumble between a grizzly bear and her cubs—be afraid, be very afraid. If you are attempting to cook dinner, visualize the bear, then chill out already. Cooking should be a pleasure. If it isn't, you're doing it wrong. You screwed it up? Fine, put it in the trash, start again, or order takeout. Remember what you did wrong and make it better next time. Not feeling consoled? Guests unimpressed? Visualize getting it wrong with that bear.

You can cook almost anything. There are, of course, elements of cooking that take years to perfect, and there are some awe-inspiringly talented cooks out there. But you don't need to be Usain Bolt to run 100 meters. Let me tell you this: there is nothing you can't cook if you're reasonably organized, pay attention, and take your time. I have included one *haute cuisine* recipe in this book: Pierre Koffman's Pig's Trotters (see p. 122). It's a classic, and would be marked as "Difficult" in the type of cookbook that mentions that kind of thing. Let's deconstruct "difficult." It requires you to bone a pig's trotter, keep things at the right temperature, and to put them all together in the right order. To do the latter you need to be organized, but less so than in your average working day. To keep things cool, you need to follow the recipe. Well, that is a very low bar. Now, boning a pig's trotter (see p. 272)—surely that's hard? Well, no. Other than having a sharp boning knife, you need only to take your time. Do it slowly, little by little. It may take you 30 minutes, not the 60 seconds that Pierre Koffman needs. He has boned pig's trotters thousands of times. Yours will be great.

Be prepared. Planning and preparation are half the battle and 90 percent of the actual work. Make sure you have all your ingredients and equipment before you start. Ensure that everything that can be done in advance, including chopping all those vegetables. That way, when you come to the fun part, you can relax, concentrate on it, do it well, and enjoy yourself.

Be serious about having fun. There was a television chef called Keith Floyd whom I liked very much. He wasn't the greatest cook in the world—he frequently made mistakes—and if truth be told, Keith was often a little drunk, or even a lot drunk. But he had tons of passion, he knew what he wanted to do, he had a swagger and a smile, and he was serious about having fun. And you should be, too. Try to channel the spirit of Keith Floyd whenever you are in the kitchen.

4. RESPECT YOUR TOOLS

Your knife is your friend. Knives are the most important tool that allow you to make food. You should spend as much as you can afford on knives and buy the very best, since with knives, price is often an indicator of quality. Great brands include Japanese Global knives (made like Samurai swords) and the big Germans: Zwilling Henckel and Wüsthof. You'll need a standard chef's knife, about

7 in [18 cm] long, and in addition to that it is useful to have a selection. I find regular use for the following: a large slicing knife, a boning knife, a paring knife, a carving knife, a cleaver, and a steel.

Love your knives. Don't abuse them. They are for cutting, not for opening cans or unscrewing screws, or whatever else you might get up to. Respect them; they are dangerous. Always keep them sharp and honed. A blunt knife is more dangerous than a sharp one. You'll need to buy yourself a sharpening stone and a steel.

USING A SHARPENING STONE

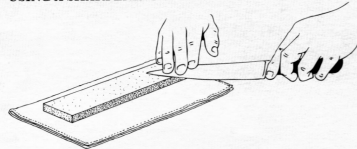

If you have a multisurface stone, start with the roughest side. Place some wet paper towels or a cloth under the stone, keeping the stone parallel with the work surface and you. Place the point of the blade in the center of the top end of the stone with your fingers.

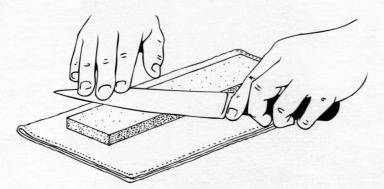

Now, applying an even pressure, push the blade along the full length of the stone at an angle of about 15°. Draw the knife from the stone cleanly and repeat a number of times to obtain a sharp edge.

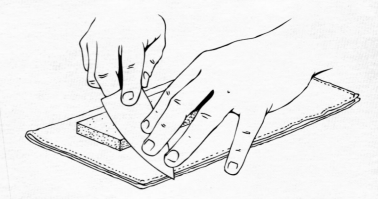

Turn the knife over and repeat the previous stages. If you are using a multisurface stone, repeat the entire process on the smoother side.

USING A STEEL
A steel will not sharpen a blunt knife, but it helps the cutting edge of a sharp knife stay sharp.

With one hand, hold the steel by the handle at a 90° angle to the work surface, with the point of the steel resting on a cloth to prevent it slipping. In the other hand, take the knife and place the base of the blade against the side farthest away from you.

Draw the blade carefully and steadily down the steel, pulling it against the steel and toward you at an angle of 15°. Repeat a number of times. Hone the entire length of the cutting edge of your knife so that you do not begin to grind a curve into your blade.

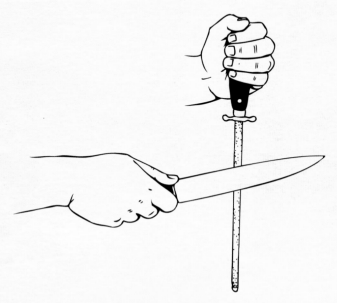

Repeat the steps above with the other side of the knife, this time starting with the knife on the side of the steel closest to you and pushing the blade away from you and down the steel simultaneously.

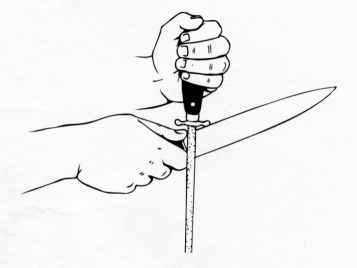

HOW TO USE THIS BOOK

This book is organized according to your situation and taste, rather than the standard Beginning, Middle, and End approach to eating. This is partly to give expression to the many facets of Manliness, and also because, quite frankly, few of us eat in the traditional appetizer-entree-dessert way any more, if indeed we ever did. The idea is that you can use the book in many ways to create a snack, a drink, or a multicourse feast.

Mostly, though, I hope the book inspires you to cook more often, and that you use and enjoy it in the same spirit of fun and exploration in which it was written. It's just a guide, and the recipes, approach, and ingredients are not carved in stone.

Get started and enjoy yourself.

CHILI & SPICE

MOZAMBICAN JUMBO SHRIMP PIRI-PIRI

INGREDIENTS (SERVES 4)

10 bird's eyes chilies, seeded

6 garlic cloves

6 Tbsp lime juice

3 Tbsp olive oil

1 tsp salt

1⅔ lb [750 g] large raw shrimp in their shells

METHOD—Preheat the oven to 350°F [180°C]. First, make your piri-piri sauce. Put the chilies on a baking sheet and roast in the oven 10 minutes. Remove and let cool a little. Remove the stalks and put in a blender along with the garlic, lime juice, olive oil, and salt. Process to a paste.

Put the shrimp in a bowl and toss in the piri-piri sauce. Leave to marinate in the refrigerator at least 3 hours.

When you are ready to cook the shrimp, light the barbecue or heat a ridged grill pan. If you are cooking indoors, make sure the room is well ventilated, as the chili fumes are quite aggressive. Thread the shrimp onto skewers. Be careful: you are handling raw chili, so it's best to wear rubber gloves. Cook 3 minutes on each side on a hot barbecue or ridged grill pan. Serve with rice.

CHICKEN JALFREZI

INGREDIENTS (SERVES 4)

2 Tbsp vegetable oil

4 garlic cloves, finely chopped

4 green chilies, chopped

3 tsp ground cumin

3 tsp ground coriander

2 tsp fresh ginger root, finely grated

14 oz [400 g] tomatoes, skinned, seeded, and chopped

1⅔ lb [750 g] chicken breasts, skin removed and cut into large chunks

2 tsp turmeric

½ tsp chili flakes

1 tsp salt

3 Tbsp clarified butter

1 large onion, thickly sliced

1 green bell pepper, deseeded and cut into strips

3 Tbsp natural yogurt

Juice of 1 lime

2 Tbsp fresh cilantro leaves

Jalfrezi means, roughly, dry or hot fry—and that gives you a clue as to what you want it to look like at the end of cooking: quite dry with a thick sauce.

METHOD—Heat the oil in a large skillet and add the garlic, chilies, cumin, coriander, and ginger. Fry 1 minute, then add the tomatoes. Cook over high heat, stirring constantly, 5 minutes. When the sauce is fairly dry, add the chicken, turmeric, chili flakes, and salt. Cook 2 minutes, stirring. Add about ½ cup [125 ml] water, cover with a lid, and cook 20 minutes, stirring occasionally.

Meanwhile, heat the clarified butter in another pan and fry the onion and green bell pepper over medium heat 15 minutes. Once the peppers have colored a little, add a splash of water.

Once the chicken has cooked, stir in the onion-pepper mixture, add the yogurt and lime juice, and stir well. Cook 5 more minutes. Sprinkle over the cilantro leaves and serve with rice or naan bread.

THAI GREEN CURRY

INGREDIENTS (SERVES 4)
PASTE:
3 lemongrass stalks, outer leaves removed, chopped

2 in [5 cm] fresh galangal, peeled and chopped (substitute with fresh ginger root if you can't find galangal)

2 shallots, chopped

20 green bird's eye chilies, seeded and chopped

5 garlic cloves, chopped

1 tsp shrimp paste

Juice of 2 limes

5 Tbsp chopped fresh cilantro leaves

½ tsp ground black pepper

Salt

CURRY:
7 Tbsp coconut cream

¾ cup [175 ml] chicken stock (see p. 245)

1 Tbsp Thai fish sauce (nam pla)

6 kaffir lime leaves

½ tsp palm sugar, or superfine if unavailable

10½ oz [300 g] chicken breast, skin and bone removed, cut into pieces

1 Tbsp shredded Thai basil (or ordinary basil)

Thai food famously combines sweet, sour, hot, and salty flavors. Outside Thailand, though, the sweet often drowns out the rest, and the hot is sometimes dispensed with entirely. This curry is a spicy, zingy corrective.

METHOD—Grind all the paste ingredients together using a mortar and pestle. You want to form a good, smooth paste. Alternatively, use a food processor. When working with this much chili, take care not to touch your eyes and wash your hands thoroughly afterward. Unless you are using the paste immediately, transfer to an airtight container.

Put the coconut cream in a saucepan and bring to a boil. Simmer 5 minutes and add 4 Tbsp curry paste. Simmer a couple more minutes, stirring well.

Add the stock, fish sauce, lime leaves, and sugar and bring to a boil. Put the chicken pieces in. Simmer about 20 minutes, or until the chicken is cooked through. If the curry is looking a little dry, add some water at this point. Taste it and judge for yourself if any of the four flavors are out of balance. Too hot? Add a little more coconut. Too creamy? Add a little more paste. If you do, give it a few minutes to cook together. Last but not least, stir in the basil and serve with rice.

HOT & SPICY DUCK RAMEN

INGREDIENTS (SERVES 4)

6½ cups [1.5 L] chicken or pork stock (see p. 245),
   or a combination

3 star anise seeds

4 duck breasts

1 Tbsp groundnut oil

14 oz [400 g] ramen noodles, fresh or dried

2 tsp shichimi togarashi

1 large red onion, thinly sliced

4 large red chilies, sliced

4 handfuls baby spinach

4 handfuls bean sprouts

4 tsp fresh cilantro leaves, chopped

1 lime, cut into wedges

Salt

METHOD—Bring a pan of salted water to a boil and heat the chicken or pork stock in another pan with the star anise.

Season the duck breasts with salt on both sides. Heat a skillet with the oil and fry the duck breasts, skin-side down, 5 minutes on each side. Remove from the pan, cover with foil, and set aside to rest.

Cook the ramen noodles in the boiling water for 3 minutes if fresh; if dried, check the instructions on the packet. Drain and place in 4 large soup bowls with ¼ tsp shichimi at the bottom of each one. Ladle the hot stock over. Check the seasoning and add salt if necessary.

Thinly slice the duck breasts and place on top of the noodles. Add the sliced onion, chilies, spinach, bean sprouts, and cilantro. Serve with lime wedges.

PEPPERED BEEF STIR-FRY

INGREDIENTS (SERVES 4)

7 Tbsp [100 ml] vegetable oil

1⅛ lb [500 g] beef steak, cut into thin strips

10 small shallots, chopped

2 Tbsp chopped fresh ginger root

5 fresh red chilies, finely chopped

10 garlic cloves, finely chopped

8 Tbsp dark soy sauce

3 Tbsp sugar

3 Tbsp black peppercorns, crushed

1 bunch scallions, cut into chunks

METHOD—Heat the oil in a large skillet or wok, add the beef, and fry on all sides. Cook 4 minutes, then remove from the pan and set aside. Return the pan to the heat, add the shallots, ginger, chilies, and garlic, and stir-fry at least 10 minutes, or until very soft. Add the soy sauce, sugar, and crushed peppercorns, and stir in the beef and scallions. Allow to heat through for a minute and serve immediately with rice or egg noodles.

CURRIED GOAT

INGREDIENTS (SERVES 4)

2¼ lb [1 kg] lean goat, mutton, or lamb meat, cut into 1¼ in [3 cm] cubes

Juice of 1 lime

2 Tbsp Jamaican curry powder

4 Tbsp vegetable oil

1 tsp brown sugar

4 garlic cloves, chopped

1 onion, chopped

1 red Scotch bonnet or other hot chili, chopped

2 sprigs fresh thyme (or 1 tsp dried thyme)

3 scallions, green part only, chopped

¾ cup [180 ml] vegetable stock (see p. 249), hot

2 potatoes, cut into chunks

4 tsp fresh cilantro leaves

JAMAICAN CURRY POWDER:

1½ Tbsp allspice berries

3 Tbsp coriander seeds

1 Tbsp turmeric

1 Tbsp fenugreek seeds

1 Tbsp black pepper

1 Tbsp ground ginger

1 cinnamon stick

1 Tbsp red chili powder

If you're put off by goat, don't be. It is utterly delicious and tender cooked this way. If you can't get hold of goat, substitute it with mutton. If you can't get mutton, use lamb, but reduce the final cooking time by 45 minutes.

METHOD—First, prepare the curry powder: put the spices in a hot, dry pan over medium heat and toast them 3 minutes, stirring frequently. Be careful not to burn them. Grind them to a fine powder with a spice grinder or a mortar and pestle. Set aside.

Place the meat in a large bowl, add the lime juice and curry powder and stir well. Cover with plastic wrap and leave to marinate in the refrigerator 6 hours.

Heat a large casserole with the oil until it is very hot. Add the goat and fry the chunks until they are browned on all sides—about 5 minutes. Reduce the heat and cover, then cook gently 30 minutes.

Remove the lid, increase the heat, and add the sugar, garlic, onion, chili, thyme, and scallions. Cook 5 minutes, until softened. Add ½ cup [120 ml] hot stock or water. Cover and simmer over a gentle heat 2½ hours, adding more stock if needed. Add the potatoes and a little more liquid and cook 15 minutes. Scatter with cilantro leaves and serve with rice and peas.

SICHUAN HOTPOT

This regional Chinese fondue is a dish to knock your socks off. It starts off hot and becomes ludicrously so by the end. Despite the pain, it is hugely addictive. Apart from the spice broth, there are no fixed ingredients. You don't need a traditional coal-burning hotpot cooker; gas and electric ones are cheaply available. Additional equipment needed for the night includes towels to wipe off your sweat and an ample supply of cold beer.

INGREDIENTS (SERVES 6)

SPICE PASTE:

- ¼ cup [50 g] fermented black beans
- 7 Tbsp [100 ml] rice wine (or medium-dry sherry)
- 4½ Tbsp [70 ml] vegetable oil
- ¼ cup [50 g] dried chilies (preferably Sichuan), soaked and chopped
- 1¼ in [3 cm] fresh ginger root, sliced
- 4 garlic cloves, sliced
- 2 Tbsp amber sugar crystals (rock sugar)
- 2 star anise seeds
- 1 Tbsp Sichuan peppercorns, crushed
- 4 cardamom pods
- 1 cinnamon stick

HOTPOT:

- 3 qt [3 L] chicken or beef stock (see p. 245)
- Fresh ginger root, sliced (optional)
- Dried chilies (optional)
- Salt

TO SERVE, A COMBINATION OF:

- Beef fillet, thinly sliced
- Pork fillet, thinly sliced
- Meatballs
- Shrimp, shelled and deveined
- Baby squid, cleaned and scored with a knife
- Firm tofu, cut in chunks
- Enoki mushrooms
- Baby sweetcorn
- Noodles

METHOD—Prepare your chicken or beef stock (see p. 245).

Using a food processor or a mortar and pestle, grind the fermented black beans and 1 Tbsp of the rice wine.

Heat the oil in a skillet and add the chilies, ginger, and garlic. Soften 5 minutes before adding the bean paste purée. Cook 5 minutes more and add the sugar, star anise, Sichuan pepper, cardamom, cinnamon, and the remaining rice wine. Simmer over low heat 20 minutes, then set aside. This can be made a few days in advance and kept in an airtight container in the refrigerator, covered with a layer of oil to stop it drying out.

Prepare the ingredients you plan to cook during dinner. If using meat, slice it very thinly, which is easiest when the meat is very cold. Cut the vegetables and tofu into mouth-pleasing sizes.

Heat the stock in a Chinese fondue or hotpot cooker (alternatively, use a heavy-based casserole dish) and add the spice paste. Add extra sliced ginger and dried chilies if you like. Let simmer 1 hour until you are ready to eat. Then, taste and season it with salt and transfer the hotpot onto its base or to a camping stove and bring to a simmer at the table. Arrange the meat, fish, and vegetables on plates and let everyone dip them in the hot stock with chopsticks. Serve with simple dipping sauces. Plain soy sauce is good, but soy sauce with a little groundnut or sesame oil works too, or try peanut butter mixed with soy, hot water, and crushed garlic and ginger. Usually, the meal ends with noodles cooked in the hot stock.

BRAISED BEEF CHILI

Top chef Heston Blumenthal makes an excellent chili con carne . . . but it takes three days. This chili is a much-simplified, magpie version, borrowing some of his good ideas (the brining and the slow braising). However, it's still quite a lengthy process. If you don't have much time, skip the brining of the meat. Do experiment with the types of chilies you add—their versatile flavors provide the backbone of the dish.

INGREDIENTS (SERVES 8)

RIBS:

4½ oz [120 g] salt

10 beef short ribs (about 2 lb [900 g] shredded meat)

Flour, for dusting

4 Tbsp vegetable oil

3¼ cups [750 ml] dry red wine

4½ cups [1 L] beef stock (see p. 245)

CHILI:

5 tsp hot chili powder, or to taste

1 tsp smoked sweet paprika

4 whole star anise seeds

2 large onions, finely diced

1 tsp brown sugar

4 red peppers, sliced

6 garlic cloves, finely chopped

2 carrots, finely diced

2 dried chipotle chilies, soaked in warm water

2 dried ancho chilies, soaked in warm water

4 dried cascabel chilies, soaked in warm water

2 Tbsp tomato paste

1¼ cups [300 ml] Bourbon

1¾ lb [800 g] canned kidney beans, washed and drained

Butter, to serve

Salt and black pepper

METHOD—Start by brining the short ribs. Mix 6½ cups [1.5 L] water in a large container with the salt, stir until dissolved, and add the short ribs. Cover and refrigerate 3 hours. Once the beef has been brined, remove it from the water, rinse well, and pat dry with paper towels.

Dust the ribs on all sides with flour. Heat the oil in a large casserole dish. When the oil is smoking hot, add the ribs. Fry on each side 1 to 2 minutes, until golden brown. Remove from the pan and set aside. Preheat the oven to 300°F [150°C].

Pour in the wine and bring to a boil, scraping the bottom of the pan. Reduce the wine by half. Return the short ribs to the pan and add the beef stock. Cover with aluminum foil and cook in the oven 4 hours.

Remove the short ribs and pull the meat off the bone. Remove any big lumps of fat. Shred the meat with a fork into long pieces and set aside. Discard the bones. Skim off any fat from the braising liquid and reserve it. Pour the liquid over the short ribs. Cover and set aside until ready to use.

To cook the chili, place a large pan over low heat and add a few spoons of the reserved beef fat. Add the chili powder and paprika and fry 1 minute. Add the star anise, onions, brown sugar, and peppers to the pan and cook 10 to 15 minutes, until softened. Then add the garlic, carrot, and drained chilies and cook 5 minutes. Add the tomato paste and cook a further 3 minutes. Increase the temperature to medium and carefully add the Bourbon (watching out in case it catches fire). Bring it to a boil and stir well.

Now add the shredded short-rib meat and its liquid to the pan. Stir in the kidney beans, cover, and simmer over low heat 90 minutes, stirring occasionally. If necessary, top up with stock or water. Season with salt and pepper. Finally, add a knob of butter. Serve with sour cream and rice.

FIERY FISH STEW

This is a wonderful recipe from Vasto, a town on the Italian Adriatic coast. A former paupers' dish, it is unusual in its utter simplicity—no water, no wine, no frying is needed. Even the addition of tomatoes or chilies was originally merely a seasonal treat. You can substitute other fish, but mussels and clams are obligatory.

INGREDIENTS (SERVES 4)

2¼ lb [1 kg] mixed fish and shellfish (such as scorpion fish, gurnard, red mullet, squid, octopus, monkfish, cuttlefish, shrimp, spiny lobster), gutted and scaled

10½ oz [300 g] clams and mussels, soaked and drained

½ cup [120 ml] olive oil

3 garlic cloves, coarsely chopped

10 fresh red chilies, coarsely chopped

7 Tbsp [100 ml] red wine vinegar

7 oz [200 g] cherry tomatoes (optional)

4 tsp fresh flat-leaf parsley, leaves chopped

Salt and black pepper

METHOD—Rinse the fish and crustaceans. Trim them, but keep their heads in place. Cut the larger ones into pieces, keeping the smaller ones (such as red mullet) intact. Clean the clams and mussels by soaking them in salt water for a while before washing them again. Ensure they are sand-free.

Heat the oil in a heavy-based casserole dish (ideally, use a clay pot, which is traditional). Add the garlic and chilies. Cook them over medium heat 10 minutes, until the chilies are browned. Remove from the heat and remove the chilies from the oil. Destalk them and put in a mortar. Pound them with a pestle and add the vinegar little by little to obtain a smooth paste. Put the pan with the garlic and oil over high heat and add the chili paste. Cook 1 minute. If using tomatoes, add them now and cook 4 minutes.

Add the fish pieces, starting with the larger ones, followed by the smaller ones, then the crustaceans, clams, and mussels. Reduce the heat to very low. Season with salt and pepper, add the chopped parsley, and gently shake the pot. Don't stir it. Cover and simmer gently 25 minutes, without stirring. To serve, very carefully remove the cooked fish, trying not to let it fall apart. Serve with toasted bread.

LAMB SHANK VINDALOO

INGREDIENTS (SERVES 4)
MARINADE:
- 1 cinnamon stick
- 4 cardamom pods
- 5 cloves
- 1 tsp mustard seeds
- 1 tsp coriander seeds
- 1 tsp fennel seeds
- 1 tsp cumin seeds
- 1 tsp black peppercorns
- 4 tsp Indian hot chili powder
  (or other hot chili powder)
- 6 dried Kashmiri chilies
  (or other large, mild variety)
- 6 garlic cloves
- ¾ in [2 cm] fresh ginger root
- ½ tsp sugar
- 3 Tbsp white wine vinegar
- 3 Tbsp white wine (optional; can be replaced
  by coconut milk or feni)

VINDALOO:
- 4 lamb shanks
- 2 star anise pods
- 3 Tbsp vegetable oil
- 1 large onion, finely chopped
- Salt

This is an extremely hot curry, but it's also full of flavor. Vindaloo is genuine, wonderful fusion food, having begun in Portugal, traveled to India, and then back again across the world over 500 years. My version combines the vinegar from the original with the heat of a modern curry, and puts the meat center stage, where it should be.

METHOD—Combine the spices, garlic, ginger, and sugar with vinegar and wine and let the ingredients soak 30 minutes before puréeing them in a blender to a fine paste.

Put the lamb shanks, star anise, and the marinade in a large bowl and leave to marinate at least 4 hours in the refrigerator.

After marinating, heat the oil in a large casserole, add the onion, and fry until soft. Add the lamb along with the marinade paste and let the spices soften and the vinegar evaporate over high heat for 5 minutes. Cover with a lid, reduce the heat, and season with salt. Add a little water if necessary to just cover the meat, and let it simmer about 90 minutes, or until tender. Serve with basmati rice.

THE ONE & ONLY BURGER

The secret of a great burger is to use good-quality meat with a high fat content, season with salt, and to cook it over high heat until well charred outside and rare in the middle. That's it. Marrow and shallots are optional. Anything else is gilding the lily.

INGREDIENTS (MAKES 6)

3 pieces veal marrow bone, about 1⅛ lb [500 g]

1¾ lb [800 g] ground chuck steak (ask the butcher to grind it for you)

2 small shallots, finely chopped

1 quantity Burger buns (see p. 265)

Your choice of toppings, to serve

Salt and black pepper

METHOD—Scrape the bone marrow out of the bones and finely chop it. Combine the marrow with the ground meat and chopped shallots in a bowl. Season with salt and pepper. Shape into patties about 2 in [5 cm] thick and press an indentation into the middle of each one with your thumb. Preheat the grill or barbecue to a high heat and cook on each side 4 minutes for medium-rare. Turn the burger once only.

AUSSIE "THE LOT" BURGER

The Australian burger has all the toppings. And then some.

INGREDIENTS (MAKES 4)

BURGERS:

1⅛ lb [500 g] lean ground beef

4 tsp Worcestershire sauce

ASSEMBLY:

4 slices Cheddar cheese

4 Burger buns (see p. 265)

8 rashers bacon

Vegetable oil, for frying

4 eggs

Butter, for spreading

Lettuce leaves, to serve

4 pineapple slices (optional)

1 large onion, thinly sliced

8 pickled beet slices

1 large tomato, sliced

Salt and black pepper

METHOD—Combine the ground beef with the Worcestershire sauce in a bowl and season with salt and pepper. Shape into 4 patties, 2 in [5 cm] thick, and press each one with your thumb to make an indentation in the middle.

Preheat the grill or barbecue to high heat and cook the burgers 4 minutes each side for medium-rare. Place a slice of Cheddar on each one for the last minute of grilling, so that it melts slightly. Remove and set aside in a warm place.

Slice the burger buns in halves and toast them on the grill. Put the bacon rashers on the grill and cook 2 minutes on each side.

While the burgers are grilling, heat a skillet with a little oil over high heat and fry the eggs, sunny side up, 3 minutes. Season with salt and pepper.

To assemble, lightly butter the buns, place a lettuce leaf on top, followed by the pineapple (if using), beet, tomato, onion, bacon, and finally the burger with the cheese and then the egg. Serve with mustard and ketchup.

FLAMED SEA BASS

This beautiful flambéed fish is a showstopper.

INGREDIENTS (SERVES 2)

1 x 2¼ lb [1 kg] sea bass, scaled and cleaned, with fins trimmed

6 fennel bulbs

3 Tbsp olive oil, plus extra for brushing

Juice of 1 lemon

Small handful dried fennel stalks (optional)

¼ cup [60 ml] pastis, or other anise-flavored spirit

Salt and black pepper

METHOD—Wash the fish and pat it dry inside and out with paper towels. Make 3 or 4 diagonal incisions about ¼ in [5 mm] deep on each side of the fish and season with salt and pepper.

Remove the fronds from the fennel and chop. Insert them in the fish's cavity. Remove the outer layers of the fennel bulbs, trim them at both ends and slice thinly.

Heat half the oil in a skillet over high heat and add the fennel. Cook for a few minutes until the fennel starts to brown. Add a splash of water, reduce the heat, and cover. Cook 5 minutes, or until the fennel is tender and the liquid has evaporated.

Heat the barbecue to medium heat. If you have dried fennel stalks, place them directly on the burning coals. Brush the fish with a little olive oil on each side and place it directly on the grill, then cook about 8 minutes on each side, or until cooked through. Put the lid on the barbecue during cooking if you have one—if not, cover loosely with aluminum foil.

Put the cooked fennel on a serving platter. Drizzle with a little lemon juice and olive oil. Once the fish is cooked, put it on the fennel bed. Put the pastis in a metal ladle and warm it over the barbecue. Carefully ignite it and pour over the fish, standing well back. Leave to flambé until the flame dies, then serve at once. Drizzle with more oil and lemon juice to serve.

GRILLED CORN
WITH SALT, CHILI & LIME

The addition of lime and chili to taste makes this simple snack somewhat addictive.

INGREDIENTS (SERVES 4)

8 corn on the cobs, preferably with husks intact

3 tsp salt

1 tsp chili flakes, or to taste

4 limes, cut into wedges

METHOD—Heat the barbecue or a ridged grill pan to medium hot. If your corns have husks, leave them on, but remove the silky threads between the husk and the corn. Place the corn cobs on the grill. Cook about 10 minutes, turning regularly—you're looking for a slightly charred, burned look. While they are cooking, mix the salt and chili flakes together. When the corn is cooked to your liking, peel back any remaining husks. Squeeze lime juice generously all over and sprinkle with the chili salt.

GRILLED PORTOBELLO
MUSHROOMS

INGREDIENTS (SERVES 4)

10 portobello mushrooms

⅜ cup [90 ml] olive oil

Juice of 1 lemon

1 garlic clove, crushed

4 tsp fresh flat-leaf parsley, leaves finely chopped

Salt and black pepper

METHOD—Clean the mushrooms by wiping them with damp paper towels; remove the stems. Mix the oil, lemon juice, garlic, and parsley together in a bowl, season with salt and pepper and add the mushrooms. Marinate 20 minutes.

Heat the barbecue or a ridged grill pan to medium hot. Put the mushrooms on the grill, gill-side down, and cook 4 minutes, then turn and cook 4 minutes on the other side. Put them on a serving plate and drizzle with a little of the remaining marinade.

JERK CHICKEN

INGREDIENTS (SERVES 4)

Juice of 1 lime

1 x 3 lb [1.5 kg] chicken, jointed into 8 pieces

JERK SEASONING:

2 Tbsp dried thyme

1 Tbsp dried rosemary

2 bay leaves, broken into small pieces

4 tsp ground allspice

1 tsp ground cinnamon

1 Tbsp black pepper

1 Tbsp brown sugar

2 tsp salt

2 garlic cloves, finely chopped

3 Scotch bonnet chilies, seeded and finely chopped

1¼ in [3 cm] fresh ginger root, peeled and grated

1 onion, finely chopped

Juice of 1 lime

4 Tbsp olive oil, plus extra for brushing

This blackened chicken looks pretty basic—and it's easy to make—but the flavor combination of pungent allspice and hot chili is fantastic, and quite unlike anything else.

METHOD—Squeeze the lime juice over the chicken and pat dry with paper towels. Slash the skin on each piece a few times with a knife. Put all the ingredients for the seasoning in a food processor and process to a dryish paste. Add a little more lime juice and oil if it does not hold together enough. Wearing gloves, coat the chicken pieces well in the jerk marinade and marinate in the refrigerator 4 hours.

Remove from the refrigerator and let the chicken come to room temperature while you prepare the barbecue with indirect and direct medium heat in places (see p. 266). Once the barbecue is very hot, lightly oil the grill and cook the chicken pieces, skin-side down, over the direct heat until seared (about 3 to 5 minutes), then move to the indirect heat part of your barbecue. Cover and cook about 25 minutes, turning several times, or until the juices run clear.

ARGENTINIAN MIXED GRILL

The *asado* is Argentina's national dish. It's a social occasion, just like barbecue the world over. What's different is the cooking method. Meats are cooked long and slow over low indirect heat, or at some distance from the coals. No rare steaks here. You can mimic this on a home barbecue in a number of ways. First, let your embers cool down and spread them thinly on the floor of your barbecue. You can top these up from time to time. Second, lift the meat up as far from the heat source as you can on your barbecue. Lastly, you can create an indirect heat zone where there are no coals in a portion of your barbecue. This will slow the cooking. The meat should not be marinated, but salt should be used liberally during cooking.

You have to have steak. Choose steak that is well marbled or from a hard-working part of the animal—rump and skirt work well. Beyond this there are no hard-and-fast rules, except that there must be lots of meat. Common additions include chorizo, morcilla and *chichulina* sausages, pork or beef ribs, and various types of offal.

Last but not least, you need the ubiquitous and delicious *chimichurri* sauce to go with all of the above.

CHIMICHURRI SAUCE

INGREDIENTS (SERVES 6)

¼ cup [60 ml] red wine vinegar
4 garlic cloves, crushed
½ tsp dried chili flakes
1 tsp salt
2¼ oz [60 g] fresh flat-leaf parsley, finely chopped
2 Tbsp fresh cilantro, finely chopped
1 Tbsp fresh oregano, finely chopped
⅝ cup [150 ml] good-quality olive oil

METHOD—Mix together the vinegar, garlic, chili, and salt in a bowl and leave to stand 20 minutes. Then, stir in the herbs and whisk in the olive oil.

This is a fresh sauce and won't keep for very long, but it will last a couple of days in a sealed jar in the refrigerator.

BARBACOA

Before barbecue, there was *barbacoa*. The ancient art of Mexican pit cooking requires a pit, embers, some liquid, and marinated meat wrapped in banana leaves, covered and left to braise for several hours. It is possible to recreate the meltingly tender meat on a barbecue, provided you have a lid. This recipe uses lamb, although you could use brisket, beef ribs, or, more authentically, a cow's head.

INGREDIENTS (SERVES 6)

1⅛ lb [500 g] chipotle in adobo (see p. 257)

4½ lb [2 kg] lamb shoulder, on the bone

1 garlic clove

1 Tbsp lime juice

1 tsp ground cinnamon

6 dried avocado leaves (optional)

Banana leaves, for wrapping

1 quantity tortillas (see p. 264)

SALSA:

3 tomatoes, chopped

2 Tbsp fresh cilantro, chopped

1 onion, chopped

Juice of 2 limes

Salt and black pepper

Lime wedges, to serve

METHOD—Put the chipotle in adobo with the garlic, lime juice, and cinnamon in a blender and process until smooth, adding some water if necessary. Liberally apply it to the lamb shoulder and let marinate overnight. The next day, place the meat with all of its marinade onto the banana leaves. Add the avocado leaves (if using) and wrap the meat in banana leaves, then in aluminum foil, and pierce the bottom several times.

Soak 6 chunks of wood, ideally hickory or oak, or an equivalent amount of chips, in water for 30 minutes.

Prepare the barbecue for a low indirect heat (see p. 266) (you're aiming for a temperature of 300°F [150°C]). Push the coals to one side and put an aluminum can filled with water next to them. Put 2 chunks of the soaked wood directly on the burning coals. Put the meat parcel on the grill on the section above the water. Close the lid and leave to smoke. Add a new wood chunk every hour, and coals as needed, and regularly replenish the water. Cook at least 6 hours, until the meat is falling off the bone. You can also do this in the oven, with a roasting tray full of liquid underneath, but you will not achieve the smoky flavor. To make the salsa, stir together all the ingredients in a bowl and season with salt and pepper. Serve the meat with tortillas, lime wedges, and salsa.

SPATCHCOCKED QUAILS

INGREDIENTS (SERVES 4)

8 quails
Salt and black pepper

GLAZE:

6 Tbsp pomegranate molasses
2 tsp ground cinnamon
1 tsp grated unwaxed orange zest
1 Tbsp orange juice

METHOD—Cut each quail along the backbone. Crack the breastbone by pressing down firmly on it, then nick the wings and thighs at the joints with a knife. Flatten the quails out, put them between two sheets of plastic wrap, and pound flat with a rolling pin. Season with salt and pepper.

Heat the barbecue to medium heat. Mix all the glaze ingredients together in a bowl. Brush the quails generously with the glaze; put breast-side up on the barbecue and grill 5 to 6 minutes on each side, or until cooked through. Serve with salad and flatbread.

KANSAS CITY RIBS

INGREDIENTS (SERVES 4)

2 racks pork spare ribs

4 Tbsp mustard (optional)

DRY RUB:

½ cup [100 g] brown sugar

2 Tbsp paprika

1 Tbsp cayenne pepper

1 Tbsp onion powder

1 Tbsp garlic powder

1 Tbsp salt

2 tsp black pepper

BASTE:

7 Tbsp [100 ml] cider vinegar

14 Tbsp [200 ml] apple juice

KANSAS CITY-STYLE BARBECUE SAUCE:

2 Tbsp butter

1 onion, finely chopped

2 garlic cloves, crushed

7 oz [200 g] tomato paste

3½ oz [100 g] molasses

7 Tbsp [100 ml] cider vinegar

5 Tbsp brown sugar

2 tsp chili powder

1 tsp cayenne pepper

1 tsp salt

1 tsp pepper

METHOD—Remove the membranes from the pork racks. Mix together the ingredients for the dry rub and apply generously all over the racks. If desired, thinly coat the ribs with mustard (to help the spices stick) and sprinkle again with the rub mixture.

Soak 6 chunks of hickory wood in water 30 minutes. Mix together the cider vinegar and apple juice to make the basting mixture.

Prepare the barbecue for a low indirect heat (you're aiming for a temperature of 230°F [110°C]). Push the coals to one side and put an aluminum can filled with water next to it. Put 2 chunks of the soaked wood directly on the burning coals. Put the ribs meat-side down on the grill on the section above the water. Close the lid of the barbecue and smoke for the first hour. Remove the lid, turn the meat, and baste it with the cider mixture. Add a new wood chunk every hour, and additional coals as needed. Turn and baste the meat every hour, and cook 4 to 5 more hours (5 to 6 hours total grilling time).

Meanwhile, prepare the barbecue sauce. Melt the butter in a saucepan. Add the onion and cook over low heat 4 minutes, or until soft. Add the garlic and cook a further minute before adding the tomato paste, molasses, vinegar, sugar, chili, cayenne pepper, and salt and pepper. Add about 7 Tbsp [100 ml] water. Stir to combine and bring to a boil. Simmer over low heat 30 minutes, topping up with water if necessary. Set aside until ready to use.

When the meat has shrunk in several places by at least ⅜ in [1 cm] and the rack is slightly bendy, apply the barbecue sauce to the racks on both sides and grill another 30 minutes. Remove from the grill, slice, and serve.

TEXAS-STYLE BEEF RIBS

INGREDIENTS (SERVES 6)

1 rack beef ribs (about 12 ribs)

1¼ cups [300 ml] beef stock (see p. 245), warm

DRY RUB:

4 Tbsp brown sugar

6 Tbsp chili powder

1 Tbsp salt

1 Tbsp black pepper

2 Tbsp paprika

2 Tbsp cayenne pepper

2 Tbsp garlic powder

GLAZE:

8¾ oz [250 g] honey

1¼ cup [250 g] brown sugar

METHOD—Combine the ingredients for the dry rub in a bowl and generously apply all over the rack of beef ribs. Let stand 1 hour. Soak some hickory chips in water 30 minutes.

Prepare the barbecue for low indirect heat (you're aiming for a temperature of 230°F [110°C]). Push the coals to one side and put an aluminum can filled with water next to them. Put a couple of handfuls of the soaked chips directly onto the burning coals.

Put the ribs meat-side down on the grill on the section above the water. Close the lid and smoke 3 hours, turning twice. Add a handful of chips every hour, as needed. Transfer the ribs to a large tray, add some warm beef stock, and cover with aluminum foil. Continue smoking for 2 to 2½ hours.

Meanwhile, combine the honey and sugar for the glaze.

When the rib bones are easily twisted and pulled out, remove from the tray and brush them liberally with the honey and sugar mixture. Put them on the grill over the direct heat and grill 5 minutes. Turn over, apply more glaze, and grill 5 more minutes. Slice the racks into individual ribs and serve.

LOBSTER
ON THE HALF SHELL

INGREDIENTS (SERVES 4)

4 x 1⅛ lb [500 g] live lobsters,
   placed in the freezer 30 minutes

3 Tbsp lemon juice

6 Tbsp [80 g] butter

3 garlic cloves, chopped

2 fresh red chilies, chopped

1 Tbsp fresh flat-leaf parsley, leaves chopped

Salt and black pepper

METHOD—Prepare the barbecue for medium direct heat (see p. 266).

Split the lobsters in half lengthwise. Remove the little sac in the head. Crack the claw shells but don't break them open completely. Season the flesh side of the lobster with salt, pepper, and half the lemon juice.

Melt the butter in a saucepan and add the garlic and chilies. Cook 1 minute, then remove from the heat.

Brush the lobsters with some of the garlic butter on both sides. Put flesh-side down on the grill 4 to 5 minutes. Turn and cook a further 4 to 5 minutes. Meanwhile, mix together the remaining garlic butter with the parsley and remaining lemon juice.

Put the lobsters flesh-side up on a serving plate and drizzle each half with sauce. Serve immediately.

PERUVIAN ANTICUCHOS

Not for the faint of heart.

INGREDIENTS (SERVES 12)

1 ox heart (alternatively, use 4½ lb [2 kg] sirloin steak)

MARINADE:

⅝ cup [150 ml] red wine vinegar

3 garlic cloves, crushed

4 tsp ground cumin

1 aji panca chili, soaked and chopped (alternatively, use
   1 tsp hot paprika)

1 tsp salt

1 Tbsp fresh flat-leaf parsley, leaves chopped

14 Tbsp [200 ml] olive oil, plus extra for brushing

DIPPING SAUCE:

2 yellow bell peppers

2 Tbsp white wine vinegar

4 Tbsp lime juice

2 garlic cloves, finely chopped

2 tsp ground aji amarillo or hot paprika

2 Tbsp olive oil

Salt and black pepper

METHOD—Wash the ox heart and remove any fat, tendons, or membranes. Cut it into 1¼ in [3 cm] thick slices; cut the slices into 1½ in [4 cm] pieces.

Combine all the ingredients for the marinade and add the meat. Coat well, cover with plastic wrap, and marinate in the refrigerator at least 3 hours.

Meanwhile, prepare the sauce. Preheat the grill to its highest setting. Halve the bell peppers and remove the stem and seeds. Brush the skins with olive oil and grill 10 to 15 minutes, until the skin is blackened all over. Remove, wrap in plastic wrap, and set aside for 10 minutes. Scrape off and discard the burned skin and chop the flesh. Put in a blender with the vinegar, lime juice, garlic, chili, or paprika and olive oil. Process, then season with salt and pepper.

Heat the barbecue to very high heat and soak some bamboo skewers 30 minutes in water. Drain the meat from the marinade and thread 3 to 4 pieces onto each skewer. Cook 1 minute, without turning, then 2 more minutes, turning frequently. Baste them several times with the marinade (be careful; this will cause a flare-up). Serve with the dipping sauce.

MOROCCAN SPICY KOFTE

INGREDIENTS (SERVES 4)

1⅔ lb [750 g] ground lamb or beef
1 onion, crushed
2 garlic cloves, finely chopped
1 tsp grated fresh ginger root
1 red chili, finely chopped
2 tsp ground cumin
1 tsp ground coriander
1 tsp ground cloves
½ tsp cayenne pepper
4 tsp fresh cilantro, leaves chopped
Olive oil, for brushing and drizzling
14 Tbsp [200 ml] Greek yogurt
3 fresh mint sprigs, leaves finely chopped
Juice of ¼ lemon
Salt and black pepper

METHOD—Put the meat in a mixing bowl and add the onion. Mix together using your hands for a few minutes, or until well combined. Add the garlic, ginger, spices, and herbs and season with salt and pepper. Mix well, cover with plastic wrap, and chill in the refrigerator 2 hours.

Soak 12 bamboo skewers 30 minutes in water. Preheat the barbecue or a ridged grill pan to medium hot. Make 12 oval-shaped sausages with the meat mixture, about 4 in [10 cm] long. Thread them onto the skewers and brush with a little olive oil. Grill, covered with the lid or aluminum foil, 6 to 8 minutes, turning once. They should release themselves from the grill easily and be nicely browned.

Mix the Greek yogurt with the chopped mint. When cooked, drizzle a little olive oil and lemon juice over the kofte and season with salt. Serve with the yogurt.

NEW ORLEANS
BARBECUED SHRIMP

They're called barbecued shrimp, but they don't actually come near a grill.

INGREDIENTS (SERVES 2)

1⅛ cup [250 g] butter, diced

1⅔ lb [750 g] large raw shrimp, shell and heads on

4 garlic cloves, crushed

2 tsp Creole hot spice mix (see p. 157)

3 tsp black peppercorns, crushed

2 Tbsp Worcestershire sauce

2 Tbsp lemon juice

Salt

METHOD—Melt a little of the butter in a skillet over high heat. Add the shrimp and fry 1 minute on each side. Add the garlic and spices and reduce the heat to medium. Fry 1 minute, then add the Worcestershire sauce and lemon juice, followed by a few butter cubes. Stir until melted and emulsified, then add a little more butter. Proceed in this manner until all of the butter is incorporated. Season with salt. Serve with fresh bread and lemon wedges.

SPICY NUTS

Football? Check. Beer? Check. Nuts? Check.

INGREDIENTS (SERVES 6)

4½ cups [500 g] unsalted mixed nuts
   (such as almonds, pecans, cashews, hazelnuts,
   walnuts, brazil nuts, peanuts)
1 Tbsp butter
3 Tbsp fresh rosemary leaves, chopped
1 tsp cayenne pepper
½ tsp chili powder
1 Tbsp salt
1 Tbsp brown sugar

METHOD—Preheat the oven to 400°F [200°C]. Put the nuts on a baking sheet and toast in the oven 5 to 10 minutes, or until golden. Turn them once or twice.

Melt the butter in a small pan. Remove from the heat and stir in the rosemary, cayenne, chili, salt, and sugar. Toss the nuts in this mixture to coat them well, and serve warm or cool.

SWEATY TACOS

These steamed, oily tacos sudados are a wonderful street food from Mexico: tasty, messy, hands-on food.

INGREDIENTS (SERVES 4)

24 corn tortillas, about 4 in [10 cm] diameter (for homemade, see p. 264)

CHILI SAUCE:

12 cherry tomatoes

Vegetable oil, for greasing

6 cascabel chilies (alternatively, use poblano chilies or another mild variety)

3 garlic cloves, halved lengthwise

1 onion, sliced

Salt and black pepper

FILLING:

8 Tbsp chipotle chilies in adobo (or see p. 257)

Juice of 1 lime

1 garlic clove, crushed

1⅓ lb [600 g] flank steak

Vegetable oil, for cooking

1 bunch fresh cilantro, roughly chopped

1 onion, thinly sliced

METHOD—Lightly brush a ridged grill pan with oil and put over high heat. Add the cherry tomatoes, cascabel chilies, garlic cloves, and onion slices until they start charring around the edges. Remove from the heat, let cool a little, then process in a food processor. Season with salt and pepper and set aside to keep warm.

To make the filling, process the chipotle chilies along with their sauce, lime juice, and garlic to a fine purée. Brush it liberally all over the steaks.

Heat a skillet with a little more oil over medium heat, and cook the steaks about 5 minutes on each side for medium-rare, or longer if desired. Leave to rest 10 minutes, then slice them thinly. Line a basket or large pot with paper towels, leaving enough overhang to completely wrap all the tacos.

If using ready-made tortillas, put them in a microwave-safe container with a damp piece of paper towel between each one and heat them 1 minute in the microwave on a low setting, or heat in a low oven. Remove and spread a spoonful of the warm chili purée over half of each tortilla. Distribute the beef filling evenly between them and sprinkle a little chopped cilantro and a few onion slices on each. Fold in half and press the edges to seal.

Brush each taco with a little vegetable oil. Layer them up inside your lined pot or basket and put a piece of baking parchment between each layer. Fold over the paper towels to cover the tacos and cover the whole thing with a lid. Put in a tamales steamer or Chinese bamboo steamer and leave to sweat at least 30 minutes.

NACHOS
WITH CHEESE
& JALAPEÑO SALSA

Even junk food is better when it's homemade junk food.

INGREDIENTS (SERVES 4)

50 tortillas (see p. 264)

Vegetable oil, for brushing

5 cups [400 g] cheese, such as Fontina, Monterey Jack, or mild Cheddar, grated

Salt

SALSA:

Juice of 2 limes

2 garlic cloves, crushed with ½ tsp salt

1 large, mild red chili, or to taste, very finely diced

2 ripe avocados, diced

1 large red onion, fined diced

1⅛ lb [500 g] tomatoes, finely diced

1 bunch fresh cilantro, chopped

2 Tbsp olive oil

¼ cup [50 g] pickled red and green jalapeño peppers, drained and chopped

METHOD

Preheat the oven to 475°F [240°C]. Brush the tortillas on both sides with oil. Stack them and cut each circle into 6 triangles. Scatter them over 2 baking sheets, season well with salt, and bake in the oven 10 minutes, or until crisp and golden. Turn them once and check them frequently so that they don't burn. Remove from the oven and let cool.

Meanwhile, make the salsa. Put the lime juice in a large bowl and add the crushed garlic. Stir well to dissolve the garlic into it, then add the chili, avocados, red onion, and tomatoes. Combine well with the lime and garlic mix. Stir in the chopped cilantro. Finally, stir in the olive oil and jalapeño peppers.

Sprinkle the grated cheese over the nachos and return the trays to the oven for 2 minutes, or until the cheese has melted. Check to make sure they don't burn.

Serve the nachos in a bowl and spoon the salsa over them, or serve the salsa separately in a bowl.

FLAMMKUCHEN

INGREDIENTS (SERVES 4)

4 cups [500 g] strong white bread flour,
   plus extra for dusting
1 tsp fast-action dried yeast
1 tsp sugar
1 tsp salt
2 Tbsp vegetable oil
7 oz [200 g] smoked bacon
2 cups [500 ml] full-fat crème fraîche or sour cream
1 tsp caraway seeds or a little grated nutmeg (optional)
1⅛ lb [500 g] onions, thinly sliced
Salt and black pepper

Literally "flame cake," this baked snack of bacon, cream, and onions from Germany and Alsace is utterly delicious.

METHOD—To make the dough, mix the flour, yeast, and sugar together in a large bowl. Dissolve the salt in 1 cup [250 ml] warm water, pour it into the flour and combine with your hands to make a rough dough. Add more water if necessary, and then the oil. Knead vigorously for 10 minutes until the dough has a very silky texture. Put in a bowl, cover with a clean dish towel, and leave to rise 2 hours in a warm place.

Once the dough has risen, preheat the oven to 500°F [260°C]. Cut the bacon rashers into thin strips. Line 2 baking sheets with baking parchment.

On a lightly floured surface, roll out the dough as thinly as possible to make 2 large rounds, and transfer them to the baking sheets. Spread the crème fraîche all over the base, season well with salt and pepper and nutmeg or caraway seeds, if using, and scatter the sliced onions all over. Sprinkle the bacon strips evenly over the top.

Bake in the oven 10 to 15 minutes, or until the edges are very crisp. Serve with a green salad.

SPRING ROLLS

INGREDIENTS (SERVES 4)

4 tsp dried shiitake mushrooms

5¼ oz [150 g] raw shrimp, shelled

5¼ oz [150 g] ground pork

2 Tbsp soy sauce

1 Tbsp Chinese rice wine

1 tsp sesame oil

½ tsp salt

2 tsp cornstarch

4 scallions, finely chopped

7 oz [200 g] cabbage, finely shredded

Vegetable oil, for frying

20 spring roll wrappers
  (available at Chinese grocery stores)

Chili sauce, for dipping (optional)

METHOD—Soak the mushrooms in boiling water to cover. Finely chop the shrimp or grind them in a food processor. Put the shrimp and pork in a bowl and add the soy sauce, rice wine, sesame oil, salt, and 1 tsp cornstarch. Mix well to combine and set aside in the refrigerator 15 minutes to allow the flavors to mingle.

Drain and chop the mushrooms and stir them, along with the scallions and cabbage, into the pork and shrimp mixture. Heat a little vegetable oil in a wok or skillet over medium heat and stir-fry the filling mixture 3 to 4 minutes, until lightly browned. Set aside to cool a little.

Meanwhile, make a paste with 1 tsp cornstarch and 1 Tbsp water. Put the spring roll wrappers on a clean work surface and put a Tbsp of the filling in the center. Dip a finger in the cornstarch mixture and use it to moisten the far edge of the wrapper. Roll up the spring roll to make a cylinder shape, tucking the sides in and sealing the edge carefully. Repeat with the rest of the mixture.

Heat enough vegetable oil for deep-frying in a large wok or deep-fat fryer to 350°F [180°C]. Deep-fry the rolls in batches until golden brown (about 5 minutes), then remove with a slotted spoon and drain on paper towels. Serve immediately, with some chili sauce to dip, if you like.

AMERICAN HOT PIZZA

This is mongrel pizza at its best: hot, greasy, and satisfying.

INGREDIENTS (MAKES 1 PIZZA)

Flour, for dusting

¼ quantity Dough (see p. 50)

4 Tbsp passata

¼ cup [50 g] pepperoni sausage, sliced

¾ cup [60 g] mozzarella, sliced

1½ oz [40 g] mixed red and green jalapeños from a jar, drained and chopped

4 tsp whole hot green pickled chilies, chopped

Olive oil, for drizzling

Salt and black pepper

METHOD—Preheat the oven to its highest setting and line a baking sheet with baking parchment. Lightly dust a clean work surface with flour and roll out the dough to a thickness of ¼ in [5 mm]. Transfer to the prepared baking sheet.

Spread the passata over the base of the pizza and season well with salt and pepper. Sprinkle the sausage, cheese, jalapeños, and chilies evenly all over it. Drizzle a little olive oil all over. Put in the oven and bake about 15 minutes, or until the cheese is bubbling and the crust is golden.

HOT WINGS
WITH BLUE CHEESE DIP

INGREDIENTS (SERVES 4)

WINGS:

7 Tbsp [100 g] butter

4 Tbsp West Indian hot pepper sauce, or to taste (see p. 250)

⅝ cup [150 g] honey

2 Tbsp red wine vinegar

24 chicken wings, cut in half across the joint

Oil, for greasing

DIPPING SAUCE:

2 cups [150 g] blue cheese, crumbled

14 Tbsp [200 ml] crème fraîche

1 red onion, finely chopped

Salt and black pepper

METHOD—Melt the butter in a small pan over low heat and add the pepper sauce and honey. Cook very gently 5 minutes, stirring well, until amalgamated. Add the vinegar, pour over the chicken wing pieces, and toss well in the mixture. Let marinate 30 minutes.

Preheat the oven to its highest setting and oil a large baking sheet. Transfer the chicken wings to the sheet and roast 20 minutes, or until cooked through and browned, turning once.

Meanwhile, make the dipping sauce. Put the cheese, crème fraîche, and onion into a bowl and crush with a fork to make a sauce. Season with salt and pepper and keep in the refrigerator until needed. Serve the chicken wings with the sauce on the side.

STICKY CHINESE SPARERIBS

Cook, gnaw to the bone. Repeat.

INGREDIENTS (SERVES 4)

1⅔ lb [750 g] pork spareribs

3 cups [700 ml] groundnut oil

MARINADE:

1 Tbsp Chinese rice wine or dry sherry

1 Tbsp light soy sauce

1 Tbsp cider vinegar

2 tsp sesame oil

1 Tbsp cornstarch

SAUCE:

2 Tbsp finely chopped garlic

2 tsp Chinese five-spice powder

3 Tbsp finely chopped scallions

3 Tbsp sugar

3 Tbsp Chinese rice wine or dry sherry

⅝ cup [150 ml] chicken stock (see p. 245)

1½ Tbsp light soy sauce

7 Tbsp [100 ml] cider vinegar

METHOD—If you have bought a rack of ribs, separate them into individual ribs by cutting vertically between them, keeping your knife close to the bone.

Mix the marinade ingredients together in a large bowl, add the spareribs, toss well to coat, and leave to steep in the marinade about 30 minutes at room temperature. Remove from the marinade with a slotted spoon.

Heat the oil in a deep-fat fryer or large wok to 350°F [180°C], or until very hot and slightly smoking. Add the marinated ribs in several batches and cook slowly until browned. Drain each batch on paper towels.

Put the sauce ingredients into a clean wok or skillet. Bring the sauce to a boil, then reduce the heat. Add the ribs, cover, and simmer gently about 40 minutes, stirring occasionally. If necessary, add a little water to the sauce to prevent the ribs from drying out. Skim any fat off the surface, turn onto a warmed serving plate, and serve at once.

DUCK BANH MI

Banh mi are the ultimate Vietnamese snack. They are usually made with small Vietnamese baguettes, which are similar to French baguettes, but made with rice flour to make them lighter and crisper. Ordinary baguettes are fine, but avoid artisan or sourdough ones—you want them crisp, not chewy.

INGREDIENTS (SERVES 2)

1 Tbsp vegetable oil

4½ oz [120 g] duck breast

2 small baguettes

2 Tbsp mayonnaise (optional)

½ cucumber, cut into thin strips

6 fresh cilantro sprigs

1 red chili, thinly sliced

1 Tbsp soy sauce

Salt

CARROT PICKLE:

2 large carrots, cut into matchsticks

1 small mooli or daikon (or ½ bunch of radishes, sliced), cut into matchsticks

2 tsp salt

½ cup [100 g] superfine sugar

1¼ cups [300 ml] rice vinegar

METHOD—To make the carrot pickle, put the carrots and mooli or daikon in a bowl with 1 tsp salt and 2 tsps of the sugar. Mix and knead with your hands about 3 minutes, pressing out any liquid (the carrots and mooli should become bendy). Drain and rinse well. Combine the rest of the sugar and salt, the vinegar, and 1 cup [250 ml] warm water and stir to dissolve the sugar. Pour over the carrots and mooli, making sure they are all submerged, and let marinate 1 hour. The pickle will keep in the refrigerator in a sealed, sterilized storage jar for up to a month.

To make the sandwich, preheat the oven or grill to its highest setting. Heat a skillet with 1 Tbsp oil. Pat the duck breast dry with paper towels and lightly score the fat with a sharp knife. Season with salt on both sides. Put in the hot pan, skin-side down. Fry over medium heat 5 minutes on each side. Transfer to the oven or grill and roast a further 5 minutes. Remove from the oven and set aside.

Split the baguettes lengthwise and remove and discard some of the dough from the insides. Sprinkle with a little water and put in the oven or grill to crisp 2 minutes. Remove and let cool before proceeding. Slice the duck into thin slices.

Generously spread the insides of the baguette with mayonnaise (if using), and add the sliced duck, cucumber, cilantro, chili, and carrot pickle in layers, sprinkling over some soy sauce occasionally. Close the sandwich firmly and cut it in half widthwise, then eat immediately.

SOUTHERN FRIED CHICKEN

This is the one dish in which MSG is a brilliant addition.

INGREDIENTS (SERVES 4)

1 chicken, jointed into 10 pieces (see p. 270)

4½ cups [1 L] milk

Groundnut or other flavorless oil, for deep frying

1 tsp dried oregano

2 tsp chili powder

2 tsp paprika

2 tsp fine sea salt

1 tsp pepper

2 tsp garlic powder

1 Tbsp dried onion flakes

2 Tbsp MSG (optional)

2½ cups [300 g] flour

2 cups [500 ml] buttermilk

METHOD—Rinse the chicken pieces and put them in a bowl with the milk. Cover with plastic wrap and chill at least 2 hours, or overnight in the refrigerator.

Transfer the chicken pieces to a large casserole dish and add the milk. Bring to a boil over medium heat and simmer gently 20 minutes. Remove the chicken pieces and drain well on a wire rack. Once the meat has drained completely (around 10 minutes), pat it dry thoroughly with paper towels.

Heat the oil in a deep-fat fryer to 350°F [180°C].

Combine the herbs, spices, salt, pepper, garlic, onion flakes, and MSG (if using) with the flour and divide the mixture between 2 separate plates. Put the buttermilk in a bowl.

Coat the chicken pieces in the seasoned flour, dip into the buttermilk, then coat in the flour mixture once more. Carefully place in the deep-fat fryer and cook in batches about 3 minutes, or until the crust is golden. Lift out with a slotted spoon and drain on paper towels.

PORK RINDS

A classic bar snack that demands to be eaten with beer.

INGREDIENTS (SERVES 4)

1⅛ lb [500 g] pork rind (preferably from the belly)

Salt

METHOD—First, dry-cure the pork rind. Score the skin diagonally in both directions at ⅜ in [1 cm] intervals. Season generously with salt on both sides, wrap in a clean cloth, and store in an airtight container in the refrigerator 48 hours.

When ready to make the rinds, pat the rind dry with paper towels and preheat the oven to its highest setting. Put the rinds on a baking sheet and roast 15 to 20 minutes, or until the skin bubbles up. The perfect rinds are crisp and deep amber colored. Watch them vigilantly to make sure they don't burn. Remove from the oven and break into pieces.

LAMB CUTLETS

Anchovy and lamb may sound like an odd couple but are, in fact, perfect companions. Trust me on this one. Ask for the cutlets to be French trimmed (in other words, with the fat and meat scraped off the long bones).

INGREDIENTS (SERVES 4)

4 Tbsp olive oil

Juice of 1 lemon

4 garlic cloves, crushed

1 fresh rosemary sprig, finely chopped

5 fresh thyme sprigs, finely chopped

16 lamb cutlets

Salt and black pepper

ANCHOVY BUTTER:

5 anchovies in oil, finely chopped

8½ Tbsp [125 g] soft unsalted butter, diced

Salt and black pepper

METHOD—Heat a heavy-based pan over very low heat and add the anchovies with 1 Tbsp of the oil in which they were packed. Encourage them to break up with a spatula. After a few minutes they should start to dissolve. Remove from the heat and pour into a bowl, season with black pepper, and set aside. When they have cooled to room temperature, add the diced butter and mix together well with a fork. Spoon the mixture onto a piece of aluminum foil and roll into a rough tube shape, twisting the ends. Put in the refrigerator to chill until you need it.

Mix together the oil, lemon juice, garlic, and herbs in a large bowl and add the lamb. If you can marinate it 30 minutes or more, all the better. If you can't wait, just turn it in the mixture so it is well covered.

Heat a ridged grill pan until hot and add the cutlets, ensuring you don't overcrowd the pan or add too much of the marinade. Season the cutlets with salt and pepper.

Cook 5 minutes on one side, then slash the fatty layer lengthwise with a small, sharp knife. This will encourage the fat to crisp up. Turn them, season again, and cook a further 5 minutes. Serve with a slice of the anchovy butter melting over the top.

PAN-FRIED SKATE
BROWN BUTTER & CAPERS

A French classic that's ready in minutes. You need one skate wing per person. The skate is best served as soon as possible after cooking, so you may want to use a couple of pans at once. Serve with new potatoes.

INGREDIENTS (SERVES 4)

4 Tbsp unsalted butter
4 skate wings, about 7 oz [200 g] each, filleted and skinned
Flour, for dusting
¼ cup [60 ml] white wine
4 Tbsp capers
Salt

METHOD—Heat a large skillet over high heat for 3 minutes. Reduce the heat to medium and add 2 Tbsp butter.

While the pan is heating, dredge the skate wings in flour and shake off the excess. Season with salt and fry them one at a time in the butter over medium heat about 2 to 3 minutes per side. Jiggle the pan when you drop them in to stop them from sticking.

Remove the skate wings and keep them warm while you add the remaining butter to the pan. Cook over medium heat until the butter turns light brown and smells nutty. Add the wine and capers. Scrape any bits that may have stuck to the bottom and simmer to evaporate the alcohol, about 2 to 3 minutes. Pour the sauce over the skate wings and serve immediately.

SALTIMBOCCA

The Italian word *saltimbocca* translates roughly as "jump in the mouth," which is certainly true of this dish, both in terms of taste and time.

INGREDIENTS (SERVES 4)

4 veal escalopes, roughly 6¼ oz [175 g] each
4 fresh sage leaves
4 slices prosciutto or other cured ham
4½ Tbsp [60 g] unsalted butter
3 Tbsp dry white wine
Salt and black pepper

METHOD—Put each escalope between 2 pieces of plastic wrap or greaseproof paper and, using a rolling pin, bash them to a thickness of no more than ¼ in [5 mm]. Season with salt and pepper. Place a sage leaf on the middle of each one and wrap a slice of ham around the whole escalope, then pin it together with a cocktail stick.

Melt the butter in a large skillet. Cook the veal over medium heat 2 minutes on each side, until golden and cooked through. Depending on the size of your pan, you may need to cook the veal in batches, in which case, just remove and keep warm while you cook the rest. Add the white wine to the pan and bubble it over high heat until thickened and reduced by half. Check the seasoning and serve the sauce poured over the escalopes.

Some people like to dust the escalopes with flour to create a thicker sauce, but please be sparing if you do. Serve with steamed new or baby potatoes and pan-fried spinach or sprouting broccoli. Add lemon juice, butter, salt, and pepper to both.

CROQUE MONSIEUR

INGREDIENTS (MAKES 2)

⅓ cup [80 ml] crème fraîche

4 thin slices good-quality white bread, crusts removed

1¼ cup [100 g] Gruyère cheese, grated

2 thin slices cooked ham, cut to the size of the bread

4 Tbsp butter

I find this a deeply comforting snack. If you want something healthy, please refer to the chapter of the same name.

METHOD—Preheat the oven to 400°F [200°C]. Spread the crème fraîche on the 4 slices of bread. Sprinkle half the cheese on 2 of the slices, then place the ham on top, followed by the other half of the cheese. Cover with the other 2 slices of bread, cream-side down. Press together firmly.

Heat the butter in a nonstick skillet. When the butter has melted, add the sandwiches and gently fry until golden, about 2 minutes on each side. Remove from the pan and put on a baking sheet. Bake in the oven 5 minutes. To serve, cut each sandwich in half and accompany with a green salad.

DEVILLED KIDNEYS ON TOAST

INGREDIENTS (SERVES 2)

6 lambs' kidneys

2 Tbsp flour

1 tsp cayenne pepper

2 Tbsp butter, plus extra for the toast

2 slices good-quality bread

4½ Tbsp [70 ml] sherry

1 tsp English mustard

Worcestershire sauce, to taste

2 Tbsp heavy cream

Salt and black pepper

METHOD—First, remove any membranes from the kidneys and cut them in half lengthwise. Cut out the little white cores. Put the flour and cayenne in a bag and season with salt and pepper. Add the kidneys, twist the bag closed, and give it a really good shake to coat them thoroughly. Remove from the flour and set aside.

Heat the butter in a skillet, and when it is sizzling, add the kidneys. Cook 2 to 3 minutes on each side, until nicely colored. Toast the bread and butter it. Add the sherry to the kidneys, and, while it bubbles, add the mustard and a few dashes of Worcestershire sauce. Cook 1 minute, then add the cream, stirring until it is well combined. Cook for a further minute and spoon over the waiting slices of buttered toast.

CALVES' LIVER, BACON & ONIONS

INGREDIENTS (SERVES 2)

2 slices calves' liver, about 5¼ oz [150 g] each

Vegetable oil, for frying

12 small onions, such as pearl or pickling onions

½ tsp powdered sugar

4 smoked bacon rashers

1 Tbsp flour

Salt and black pepper

METHOD—Remove any pieces of skin, tendons, or tubes from the liver and pat dry with paper towels. Set aside.

Heat 2 Tbsp oil in a large skillet over low heat and add the onions. Dust them with a little powdered sugar. Let the onions cook gently 20 minutes, until they are nicely browned and caramelized. Remove from the pan and keep warm. Wipe the pan clean and add 1 Tbsp oil over low heat. Add the bacon and cook on both sides until crisp, about 4 minutes in total. Remove and keep warm. Increase the heat to medium. Lightly dust the livers with the flour, shaking off any excess. Add to the pan and cook 1 to 2 minutes on each side. Season with salt and pepper and serve with the onions and bacon.

DEEP-FRIED
SALT & PEPPER SQUID

A bit more peppy than Greek-style fried calamari, but just as easy and quick.

INGREDIENTS (SERVES 4)

1⅔ lb [750 g] baby squid, each about 1½ to 2 in [4 to 5 cm] long, cleaned

1 Tbsp Sichuan peppercorns, crushed (or use black peppercorns)

1 tsp chili flakes

2 tsp sea salt

4 Tbsp all-purpose flour

4 Tbsp cornstarch

Groundnut oil, for frying

3 garlic cloves, sliced

1 red chili, seeded and sliced

4 scallions, sliced

1 lemon or lime, cut into wedges

METHOD—First, prepare the squid. Cut off the tentacles and slice the bodies into rings, about ⅜ in [1 cm] thick. Pat dry with paper towels.

In a mortar and pestle, crush together the peppercorns, chili flakes, and sea salt. Stir in the flour and cornstarch. Put the mixture in a plastic bag, add the squid rings, twist it shut, and shake well so that the squid is well coated with flour. Remove from the bag, dusting off any excess flour.

Heat the oil in a deep-fat fryer or wok to 350°F [180°C]. If using a deep-fat fryer, follow the manufacturer's instructions regarding the quantity of oil. If using a wok, fill it about one-third full with oil. The oil is hot enough when a cube of bread browns in 30 seconds. Carefully add the squid to the hot oil in batches and fry until golden, about 1 to 2 minutes.

Add the garlic, chili, and scallions to the oil and fry 20 seconds. Remove and drain the squid and flavorings and serve immediately with wedges of lemon or lime.

SINGAPORE FRIED NOODLES

This street food and takeout classic is really quick and easy.

INGREDIENTS (SERVES 2)

8 Chinese dried mushrooms

8¾ oz [250 g] rice noodles

2 Tbsp light soy sauce

2 Tbsp oyster sauce

2 Tbsp rice wine vinegar

2 Tbsp groundnut oil

5 garlic cloves, chopped

1 tsp finely chopped fresh ginger root

2 Tbsp turmeric

7 oz [200 g] water chestnuts

4 scallions, finely sliced

8¾ oz [250 g] raw shrimp, shelled and deveined

1 egg, beaten

2 Tbsp sesame oil

METHOD—Soak the Chinese mushrooms in boiling water for 20 minutes. Drain, then chop roughly and set aside. Meanwhile, cook the rice noodles in a separate pan according to the instructions on the packet, drain, and set aside.

Combine the soy and oyster sauces and the rice wine vinegar in a cup and set aside.

Heat the groundnut oil in a wok or skillet and stir-fry the garlic and ginger 1 minute. Add the turmeric, chopped mushrooms, water chestnuts, and scallions and stir well. Now add the shrimp and cooked noodles. Add the soy sauce mixture. Lastly, add the beaten egg and sesame oil, stirring gently until the egg is cooked through. Serve immediately.

SQUID & CHORIZO
WITH CHICKPEA SALAD

An alternative surf 'n' turf. Salty seafood and spicy chorizo are exceptionally good partners in this simple and instantly gratifying dish.

INGREDIENTS (SERVES 4)

1⅛ lb [500 g] squid, cleaned

Olive oil, for frying

10½ oz [300 g] spicy cooking chorizo

1 x 14 oz [400 g] can chickpeas, drained

1 large tomato, diced

1 Tbsp chopped fresh flat-leaf parsley

3 Tbsp olive oil

2 Tbsp lemon juice

1 garlic clove, crushed

Salt and black pepper

METHOD—If using large squid, slice into ⅜ in [1 cm] rings. If using baby squid, score the flesh gently with a sharp knife. Cut the tentacles in two (or leave intact if using baby squid). Dry with paper towels, then toss in a little olive oil and set aside.

If using small cooking chorizo, cut in half lengthwise; larger sausages should be cut into small chunks.

Heat a ridged grill pan until it is very hot and add the squid. Cook about 2 minutes, turning once, until just firm, then remove. Add the chorizo and cook 3 to 4 minutes, turning, until cooked. Both the squid and chorizo should have good charred marks. Set aside.

Stir together the chickpeas, tomato, and parsley in a serving bowl. Whisk together the oil and lemon juice with the garlic and a little salt and pepper and pour onto the salad. Toss and serve with the squid and chorizo.

BEEF & BLACK BEAN STIR-FRY

INGREDIENTS (SERVES 2)

- 1 tsp sugar
- 2 Tbsp oyster sauce
- 2 Tbsp soy sauce
- 2 Tbsp sesame oil
- 3 Tbsp rice wine vinegar
- 2 Tbsp groundnut oil
- 8¾ oz [250 g] beef steak, fillet or sirloin, sliced into thin strips
- 2 garlic cloves, sliced
- 2 tsp finely chopped fresh ginger root
- 1 tsp finely chopped red chili
- 1 onion, finely sliced
- 1 red pepper, finely sliced
- 1 green pepper, finely sliced
- 1½ Tbsp black beans

The secret of a good stir-fry is to prepare everything before you start cooking. The actual cooking time is really quick—just a few frenetic minutes. Resist the temptation to cook things for too long. The vegetables in particular should have a bit of bite to them.

METHOD—Mix together 14 Tbsp [200 ml] water with the sugar, oyster and soy sauces, sesame oil, and rice wine vinegar in a cup. Stir until the sugar has dissolved. Set aside.

Heat the groundnut oil in a wok or skillet and add the strips of steak. Fry 2 minutes, turning frequently. Remove and set aside in a bowl, retaining the oil in the wok.

Return the wok to the heat and add the garlic and ginger. Stir well, then add the chili. Add the onion, peppers, and black beans and cook another minute, stirring constantly. Return the beef to the pan along with any juices that have gathered in the bowl.

Finally, add your cup of sauce and cook a minute, stirring, then serve immediately over a bowl of boiled rice or noodles.

PAN-FRIED DUCK BREAST
WITH MUSTARD POTATOES

INGREDIENTS (SERVES 2)

2 duck breasts, about 10½ oz [300 g]

3 Tbsp groundnut oil

1⅛ lb [500 g] baby potatoes

2 tsp wholegrain mustard

1 Tbsp heavy cream

1½ Tbsp fresh flat-leaf parsley, chopped

Salt and black pepper

METHOD—Pat the duck breasts dry with paper towels. Score the fat in a cross-hatch pattern, without cutting into the meat, and season with salt on both sides. Set aside.

Heat the oil in a heavy-based pan over medium heat. Add the potatoes, coat well with the oil on all sides, and cover the pan. Cook about 15 minutes, or until the potatoes are tender and golden. Remove the lid, increase the heat, and fry another 10 minutes, until crispy. Add the mustard, fry another minute, then add the cream and parsley. Shake the pan well and season with salt and pepper.

While the potatoes are cooking, place a skillet over high heat until very hot. Add the duck breasts, skin-side down, and reduce the heat to medium. Fry on the skin side 8 minutes, then turn over and fry another 5 minutes. Season with salt and pepper and remove from the pan. Leave to rest 5 minutes. Once the potatoes are cooked, slice the duck breasts and serve.

PLOUGHMAN'S LUNCH

INGREDIENTS (SERVES 4)

1⅛ lb [500 g] good-quality cooked ham, cut in very
   thick slices

1 to 2 large pieces hard cheese, such as mature
   Cheddar and Stilton

1 loaf farmhouse bread, sliced

2 apples, cut into pieces

Chutney (see p. 253), to serve

Pickled onions, to serve

Mustard, to serve

PICCALILLI:

½ cup [100 g] sugar

4½ cups [1 L] cider vinegar

1 cauliflower head, broken into small florets

1⅛ lb [500 g] French beans, trimmed and cut
   into large pieces

1 cucumber, peeled and thickly diced

2 tsp mustard powder

2 tsp turmeric

1 tsp honey

2 garlic cloves, crushed

3 Tbsp white wine vinegar

9 Tbsp sunflower oil

1 red onion, sliced

Salt and black pepper

BEET SALAD:

½ tsp caraway seeds, toasted

4 Tbsp vegetable oil

2 shallots, finely chopped

4 Tbsp red wine vinegar

4 beets, boiled, skinned, and roughly chopped

Salt and black pepper

The "Ploughman's Lunch" is a traditional British dish. It is an assembly of rustic fare that is just what you need after a hard morning plowing in the fields.

METHOD—For the piccalilli, bring the sugar and cider vinegar to a boil in a pan. Add the cauliflower, the beans, and cucumber. Cook 3 minutes, then remove and drain. In a small mixing bowl, combine the mustard powder, turmeric, honey, and garlic with the white wine vinegar. Season with salt and pepper. Stir well before adding the sunflower oil. Put the onion in a bowl, add the vegetables and the dressing, and toss. Keep refrigerated and use within 2 days.

For the beet salad, toast the caraway seeds in a little vegetable oil in a hot skillet. Mix together the shallots, caraway seeds, and vinegar in a bowl and add the oil. Add the beet and stir gently.

To serve, simply assemble all the components, preferably on a wooden board. Serve with beer.

SLOW FOOD

BORSCHT WITH BEEF

INGREDIENTS (SERVES 6)

2¼ lb [1 kg] chuck steak, or other stewing meat,
  cut into 1¼ in [3 cm] cubes

1 bay leaf

1 onion, studded with 3 cloves

1 carrot

1 celery stalk

2 Tbsp vegetable oil

2 onions, chopped

3 garlic cloves, crushed

2 large tomatoes, skinned, seeded, and diced

1 Tbsp tomato paste

6 medium potatoes, peeled and quartered

3 beets, peeled and grated

3 Tbsp red wine vinegar

1⅛ lb [500 g] white cabbage, shredded

Small bunch fresh dill, finely chopped

Salt and black pepper

There are many versions of borscht; this one is a rich, heart-warming winter stew and bears little resemblance to the light, cold beet soup of the same name.

METHOD—Put the beef in a large casserole dish with the bay leaf, the onion studded with cloves, the carrot, and celery. Cover with cold water and bring to a boil. Skim off any impurities and simmer gently 2 hours.

When the beef is nearly ready, remove and discard the carrot, celery, and onion with cloves. In another pan, heat the oil and cook the onions 3 minutes. Add the garlic and cook another minute. Add the onions and garlic to the casserole with the beef, then add the tomatoes, tomato paste, potatoes, beet, and vinegar. Add the shredded cabbage and cook gently another 40 minutes. Season with salt and pepper. Add a handful of dill and serve with a dollop of sour cream and fresh bread.

AUTHENTIC BOLOGNESE SAUCE

There are many ways of making this satisfying ragù; you probably have your own. The inclusion of different ingredients is much debated, but the crucial elements for an "authentic" Bolognese sauce are the addition of milk and the lengthy cooking time. If you have never used milk, you'll find it's a revelation. The sauce tastes even better the next day, so make more than you need or plan ahead.

INGREDIENTS (SERVES 6)

3 Tbsp olive oil

1¾ oz [50 g] pancetta, finely chopped

1 onion, finely chopped

1 garlic clove, finely chopped

1 carrot, finely chopped

1 celery stalk, finely chopped

12¼ oz [350 g] ground meat (preferably a combination of veal, beef, and pork)

1 cup [250 ml] milk

14 Tbsp [200 ml] white wine

1 x 14 oz [400 g] can chopped tomatoes

1 bay leaf

Pinch of dried oregano

Salt and black pepper

METHOD—Heat the oil in a wide pan or casserole dish, add the pancetta, and cook a few minutes until it starts to crisp and the fat starts to run. Add the onion and let it soften over medium heat 2 to 3 minutes before adding the garlic, carrot, and celery. Stir the vegetables frequently for about 5 minutes, then increase the heat, add the ground meat, and cook, stirring occasionally, until the meat has browned all over. Season with salt and pepper.

Add the milk and let it evaporate completely before adding the wine. Let the wine evaporate, then add the tomatoes. Add the bay leaf and oregano, cover, and simmer very gently over very low heat about s3 hours. Stir occasionally and check regularly that there is enough liquid, adding a little water if necessary. Serve with spaghetti, or (even better) with tagliatelle.

POT-BAKED LAMB WITH ORZO

Traditionally cooked in small earthenware pots, this Greek dish is deliciously succulent. The meat falls off the bone and the orzo pasta is full of flavor.

INGREDIENTS (SERVES 6)

14 Tbsp [200 ml] olive oil

6 small lamb shanks (or 1 x 4½ lb [2 kg] leg of lamb)

Juice of 1 lemon

4 fresh oregano sprigs (or 2 tsp dried)

1¾lb [800 g] fresh tomatoes (or use canned)

1 onion, diced

4 garlic cloves, sliced

½ tsp sugar

7 Tbsp [100 ml] white wine

1 cinnamon stick

1 bay leaf

2 Tbsp butter

1⅛ lb [500 g] orzo pasta

2½ cups [200 g] kefalotyri cheese, or other hard, salty sheep's milk cheese, such as pecorino, grated

Salt and black pepper

METHOD—Preheat the oven to 300°F [150°C]. Heat half the olive oil over a high heat in a flameproof baking or shallow casserole dish, add the meat, and quickly brown it all over. Add the lemon juice and oregano and season with salt and pepper. Transfer to the oven, add a splash of water, cover with aluminum foil, and roast slowly 2 hours (or 2½ hours if using a whole leg).

Meanwhile, prepare the tomato sauce. Put the tomatoes in a heatproof bowl, cover with boiling water, and remove them after a minute or two, once the skin has cracked. Drain and let cool slightly, then peel off the skin, deseed, and chop them.

Place the remaining oil in a saucepan over medium heat. Add the onion and cook 4 to 5 minutes, or until softened. Add the garlic and sugar and increase the heat. Pour in the wine and let it evaporate. Add the tomatoes, breaking them up with a fork, then the cinnamon stick, bay leaf, and remaining oregano and season with salt and pepper. Cover and simmer gently over very low heat until ready to use. If necessary, add a little water.

When the meat is nearly ready, heat 3¼ cups [750 ml] water. Melt some butter in a skillet and fry the orzo over high heat until golden, stirring constantly, about 5 minutes. Remove the casserole from the oven and increase the temperature to 350°F [180°C]. Turn the meat over and add the orzo, the tomato sauce, and the hot water to the dish. Stir with a fork.

Return the meat to the oven, cover with aluminum foil, and bake another 1½ hours. Remove the foil and sprinkle the grated cheese over the top. Increase the temperature to 400°F [200°C]. Return to the oven and bake 15 minutes. The liquid should be completely absorbed by the orzo.

PORK BRAISED IN MILK

INGREDIENTS (SERVES 6)

2¼ lb [1 kg] pork loin

4½ cups [1 L] dry white wine

2 Tbsp butter

2 Tbsp olive oil

4½ cups [1 L] milk

6 fresh sage leaves

1 fresh rosemary sprig

Salt and black pepper

METHOD—Pat the meat dry with paper towels and put it in a bowl with the white wine. Marinate it for at least 24, preferably 48, hours in the refrigerator.

Remove the pork and pat it dry with paper towels. Truss it with kitchen string to prevent it from falling apart during cooking. Season with salt and pepper.

Heat the butter and oil in a large casserole dish and fry the pork on all sides until browned, then remove and set aside. Add 3 Tbsp of the marinade and let evaporate completely. Return the meat to the pan, pour over the milk, and add the herbs. Simmer very slowly on the lowest heat possible about 2½ hours. Baste occasionally; do not let it boil, or the milk will split. When tender, increase the heat and reduce the milk until it is quite thick. Lift off some of the pork fat with a spoon and strain the sauce. Destring the meat, slice, and serve with the sauce. Roasted potatoes (see p. 143) with rosemary are a great accompaniment.

BEEF IN GUINNESS

INGREDIENTS (SERVES 6)

3 Tbsp vegetable oil

3½ oz [100 g] lardoons

2¼ lb [1 kg] braising steak, cut into large chunks

3 onions, diced

3 carrots, sliced

5 garlic cloves, crushed

3 Tbsp flour

2 fresh or dried thyme sprigs

2 bay leaves

2 cups [500 ml] Guinness

1 cup [250 ml] beef or vegetable stock (see p. 245 to 249)

Salt and black pepper

METHOD—Preheat the oven to 300°F [150°C]. Heat the oil in a large casserole dish, add the lardoons, and fry until browned, then remove and set aside. Next, brown the beef in batches (if you overcrowd the pan, the meat may boil rather than fry). Set aside. Add the onions and cook about 5 minutes, until softened. Add the carrots and garlic and cook a further 3 minutes.

Return the beef and the lardoons to the casserole. Season with salt and pepper and sprinkle with the flour. Stir well, and after another minute add the thyme, bay leaves, Guinness, and stock. Cover and cook in the oven 3½ hours. The meat should be very tender and the sauce only faintly bitter-tasting. If necessary, cook for another hour, adding a little water if needed. Serve with potato or parsnip mash.

BEEF IN VINEGAR

Meat dishes marinated in vinegar are found in many cuisines, such as German *sauerbraten*, Goan pork vindaloo, and this Veneto version of *pastissada*, a Veronese horse meat stew with red wine. It was an excellent way of tenderizing and preserving meat before refrigeration was available. It is very flavorful and needs robust side dishes, such as polenta or German-style potato dumplings.

INGREDIENTS (SERVES 6)
MARINADE:

1 cup [250 ml] white wine vinegar

1 cup [250 ml] dry white wine

2 garlic cloves

½ cinnamon stick

2 cloves

1 fresh rosemary sprig

6 peppercorns

2 celery stalks, finely chopped

Salt

BEEF:

2¼ lb [1 kg] beef top rump, in one piece

7 Tbsp [100 g] butter

1 onion, diced

½ cup [120 ml] Marsala

½ cup [120 ml] dry white wine

Salt and black pepper

METHOD—To make the marinade, put the vinegar, wine, garlic, spices, herbs, and celery in a large bowl and season with salt. Add the beef, cover with plastic wrap, and marinate in the refrigerator a minimum of 12 hours, turning occasionally. When ready to use, remove from the marinade and pat the meat dry with paper towels. Pour the marinade through a sieve and remove the spices, but keep the rosemary, garlic, and celery. Discard the liquid and spices.

In a large casserole dish, melt the butter and fry the onion 4 to 5 minutes, until slightly softened, then add the reserved celery, garlic, and rosemary from the marinade. Cook 1 minute before adding the meat and browning it on all sides. Season with salt and pepper, then add the Marsala and white wine. Cover the meat with aluminum foil and put the lid back on. Simmer over a gentle heat 2½ hours. Remove the beef and slice it quite thickly. Arrange it on a warmed serving platter. Strain the sauce and pour it over the meat.

CASSOULET

This is a meal for a soccer team.

INGREDIENTS (SERVES 10)

BEANS:

2¼ lb [1 kg] dried white haricot beans
  (or other dried white beans), soaked overnight

2 onions

4 cloves

7 oz [200 g] fresh pork rind, blanched

1 carrot, peeled

1 bouquet garni

2 garlic cloves

10½ oz [300 g] lean pork belly

1 x 8¾ oz [250 g] raw garlic sausage

CASSOULET:

2 Tbsp duck fat

2 onions, finely chopped

6 garlic cloves, crushed

2 large tomatoes, skinned, seeded, and chopped

1¼ cups [300 ml] white wine

6 large pork sausages, preferably Toulouse

6 legs confit duck (see p. 202)

2 cups [130 g] fresh white breadcrumbs

4 tsp fresh flat-leaf parsley, leaves chopped

2 garlic cloves, finely chopped

Salt and black pepper

METHOD—Drain the beans and put them in a casserole dish with 2 onions, each stuck with 2 cloves, the pork rind, the carrot, bouquet garni, and 2 garlic cloves. Cover with cold water. When the water starts to boil, reduce the heat to low and simmer 1 hour. Add the pork belly and the raw garlic sausage and simmer another 15 minutes, then remove the sausage and pork belly. Reserve the meats and remove the other ingredients; drain the beans through a colander over a bowl, reserving the cooking liquid.

Preheat the oven to 275°F [140°C]. Heat the duck fat in a large pan and cook the onions 4 minutes, or until softened. Add the 6 crushed garlic cloves, fry 1 minute, then add the chopped tomatoes. Stir well and add the wine. Let it almost entirely evaporate before adding the cooked, drained beans. Season with salt and pepper and stir well. Add a ladle of the bean-cooking liquid and simmer 5 minutes.

Meanwhile, heat a skillet and fry the sausages until browned. Cut the cooked pork belly and the garlic sausage into 1⅜ in [1 cm] slices. Remove the confit duck legs from their fat. Set aside.

Line the bottom of an ovenproof earthenware dish or casserole with the pork rind and add half the bean-onion-tomato-mixture on top. Now add the duck legs, sliced sausage, and pork belly and the whole fried sausages on top, then another layer of beans. Add enough bean-cooking liquid to just reach the top layer of beans (but not more).

Cook in the oven 3 hours. If necessary, add a little liquid from time to time to prevent the dish from drying out. To make the topping, mix the breadcrumbs, chopped garlic, and parsley together. Sprinkle evenly on top of the cassoulet and bake another 45 minutes, or until the topping is crisp and browned. Serve piping hot.

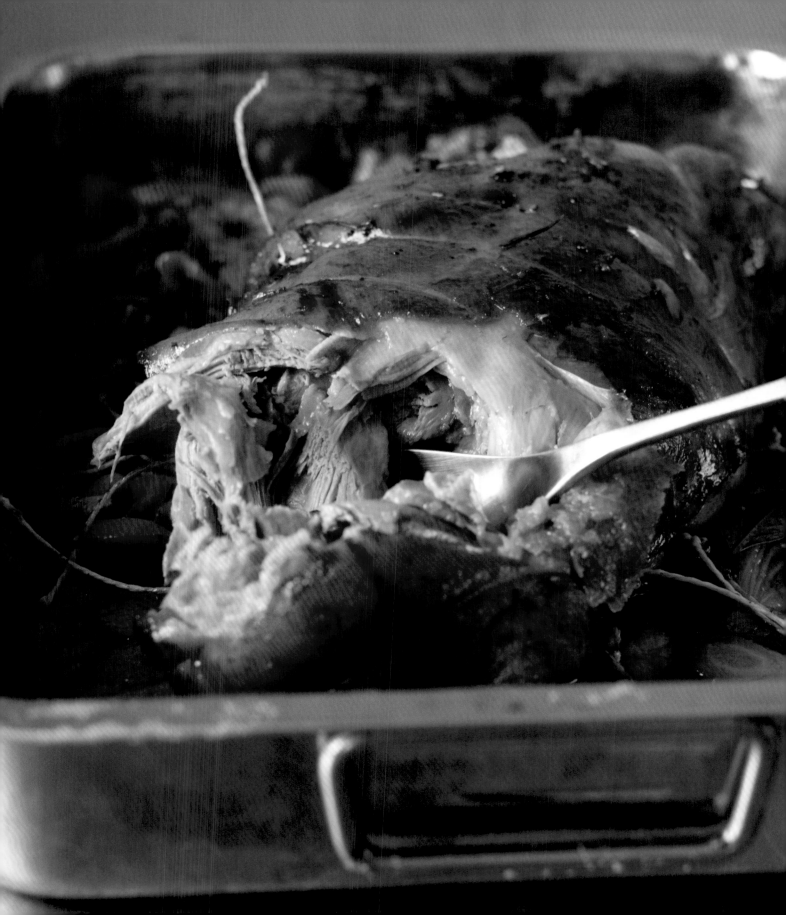

SEVEN-HOUR LEG OF LAMB

This classic lamb dish is so meltingly tender you can eat it with a spoon. It may take at least 7 hours, but it cooks itself, so you can be busy with something else in the meantime.

INGREDIENTS (SERVES 8)

1 leg of lamb, about 6½ lb [3 kg]

6 garlic cloves, thinly sliced

3 Tbsp olive oil

2 heads garlic, halved widthwise

2 onions, quartered

4 carrots, cut into large chunks

1 bouquet garni with thyme and rosemary

1 cup [250 ml] white wine

2 cups [250 g] flour

Salt and black pepper

METHOD—Preheat the oven to 300°F [150°C]. Make small incisions all over the lamb using a small, sharp knife. Push a sliver of garlic into each one. Rub olive oil all over the lamb and season with salt and pepper. Put it in a large casserole dish with the heads of garlic, onions, carrots, bouquet garni, and wine, then put the lid on.

Now you need to make a dough to seal the pan, so that the lamb remains moist. In a bowl, mix together the flour with 1 cup [250 ml] water to make a dough. Apply the dough to seal the gap between the pan and the lid. It doesn't need to look pretty, and you won't be eating it. Cook in the oven at least 7 hours, preferably 9 or 10.

At the end of the cooking time, remove the casserole from the oven and break and discard the seal before serving. At home I eat this with crispy roast potatoes (see p. 143), which provide a nice contrast of textures with the melting lamb.

ROAST GOOSE

INGREDIENTS (SERVES 8)

1 x 11 lb [5 kg] goose, giblets reserved

2 Tbsp vegetable oil

2 onions, chopped

1 celery stalk, chopped

2 carrots, chopped

1 bouquet garni

15 black peppercorns

½ tsp dried thyme

½ tsp dried marjoram

6 tart dessert apples, peeled, cored, and quartered

Salt and black pepper

METHOD—First, prepare a stock: chop the goose neck, liver, and heart, heat a little oil in a pan, and fry them with the onions. Add celery, carrots, bouquet garni, and peppercorns. Cover with cold water, bring to a boil, skim off any impurities with a slotted spoon, and simmer 2 hours. Skim off any fat and strain, reserving the liquid.

Preheat the oven to 475°F [240°C]. Rub the goose with the dried herbs and season with salt and pepper. Season the cavity and stuff it with the apples. Truss the cavity with a kitchen needle and string.

Pour 1 cup [250 ml] boiling water into a roasting tin. Put the goose breast-side down on a trivet or rack in the tin and cook in the oven 45 minutes. Once the liquid has evaporated completely, remove from the oven and prick the skin all over, especially under the wings and legs. Be very careful to only pierce the fat layer and not the meat itself. Baste the goose occasionally with its fat and juices. If a lot of fat is released, remove some of it each time. Add a few ladles of the prepared stock to the tin (don't pour it over the goose). Once the back has colored nicely, carefully turn the goose over, breast facing up. Baste it regularly and add more stock to the tin if necessary. When the goose is golden all over, turn the oven down to 375°F [190°C]. In total, the goose should cook about 3½ hours, depending on its size and age. To check if it is cooked, insert a sharp knife or skewer into the thickest part of the leg—the juices should run clear. If they are still pink, cook a little longer.

Increase the heat to 475°F [240°C] about 10 minutes before the end of cooking, and brush the goose's skin with salted water. This helps make it crisp. Remove the goose and keep warm. Loosen any bits stuck to the bottom of the tin and pour the contents of the roasting tin through a sieve into a bowl. Lift off any fat with a spoon.

Remove the apples from the cavity and place on a serving dish. Present the goose on a large platter and carve it triumphantly at the table. Serve with red cabbage, steamed potatoes, and roast chestnuts.

RED CABBAGE

INGREDIENTS (SERVES 8)

- 2¼ lb [1 kg] red cabbage
- 2 Tbsp clarified butter
- 1 Tbsp sugar
- 1 onion, finely chopped
- 3 apples, peeled and cut into large chunks
- ¼ cup [60 ml] cider vinegar
- 3 bay leaves
- 1 tsp caraway seeds
- 1 onion, studded with 4 cloves
- 2 Tbsp redcurrant jelly or fresh cranberries
- 1 cup [250 ml] dry red wine
- 1 Tbsp flour (optional)
- Salt and black pepper

METHOD—Red cabbage is best made a day in advance. Cut out the core and slice into very fine strips. Heat the butter and sugar in a large pan. When the sugar starts to caramelize, add the chopped onion and apples. Cook 1 minute, then add the cabbage, immediately followed by the vinegar. Now add the spices, whole onion, redcurrant jelly, or cranberries and wine, cover, and simmer 45 minutes. Keep a kettle filled with hot water ready. Stir the cabbage frequently and top it up with a little hot water when necessary. The cabbage should be soft, but retain a little bite. If the consistency is a little too liquid for your liking, dust the cabbage at the end with a little flour, stir well, and cook 1 minute. Season with salt and pepper. If making the day before, let cool and store in the refrigerator overnight, then reheat over low heat to serve.

COQ AU VIN

INGREDIENTS (SERVES 6)
MARINADE:

1 carrot, cut into 4 pieces

1 onion, quartered

1 celery stalk, cut into 4 pieces

8 black peppercorns

1 bouquet garni

3¼ cups [750 ml] dry red wine

CHICKEN:

1 x 4½ lb [2 kg] chicken, cut into 8 pieces

7 oz [200 g] lean bacon rashers or lardoons

8¾ oz [250 g] button mushrooms

5¼ oz [150 g] pearl onions or small shallots, peeled

4 Tbsp oil or butter

2 Tbsp brandy

2 Tbsp flour

2 garlic cloves, finely chopped

2 fresh or dried thyme sprigs

1 bay leaf

3¼ cups [750 ml] dry red wine

1 small square dark chocolate (optional)

Salt and black pepper

METHOD—Put the carrot, onion, celery, peppercorns, and bouquet garni in a bowl and add the red wine for the marinade. Add the chicken pieces, turn to coat with the marinade, cover with plastic wrap, and marinate about 24 hours in the refrigerator.

Cut the bacon rashers, if using, into fine strips. Trim the ends of the mushrooms and quarter them, if large. The small ones can remain whole. Heat a large skillet and add the bacon strips. Fry 3 to 4 minutes over medium-high heat until golden, then remove and set aside. Next, reduce the heat, add the onions, and cook gently in the bacon fat until slightly colored, about 4 to 5 minutes. Remove from the pan and set aside. Repeat with the mushrooms.

Remove the chicken pieces from the marinade and pat them dry with paper towels. Season with salt and pepper. Strain the marinade into a pan and bring it to a boil, then simmer until reduced by half.

In a large casserole dish, heat the oil or butter and quickly brown the chicken pieces over high heat, turning them regularly. Add the brandy and carefully ignite it to burn off the alcohol, keeping the lid handy to extinguish the flames if necessary. If your pan is shallow, you can do this by tilting it carefully toward the flame until the brandy ignites. Alternatively, you can heat the brandy in a metal ladle, ignite it, and then pour it over the chicken. Stand well back and wait for the flames to die down, then continue to simmer.

When the liquid has evaporated, sprinkle the flour over the chicken pieces and let it brown quickly. Return the onions and bacon to the pan along with the garlic, thyme, and bay leaf. Season with salt and pepper.

Add the reduced marinade and the second quantity of wine. Bring to a boil and simmer over low heat 1½ hours. If the wine is very acidic, you can add a little chocolate. Add the mushrooms 15 minutes before the end of cooking; the sauce should be slightly thickened by this point. If it is too liquid, mix 1 Tbsp flour with 4 Tbsp butter and dissolve it in a ladle of the sauce. Add to the casserole and stir for a few minutes, until thickened. Serve with fresh pasta, such as pappardelle.

SLOW-ROAST PORK BELLY

INGREDIENTS (SERVES 4)
2¼ lb [1 kg] pork belly
2 tsp fennel seeds
¾ cup [175 ml] dry sherry
Salt

METHOD—Using a sharp knife, cut the skin of the pork belly, without cutting into the meat, at ⅜ in [1 cm] intervals to form a cross-hatch pattern. Sprinkle a generous amount of salt on a plate and place the pork, skin-side down, onto the salt. Leave to sit in the refrigerator 2 hours before shaking any excess salt off the rind. Sprinkle the fennel seeds over the scored skin, pressing some down into the slashes you have made.

Preheat the oven to 475°F [240°C]. Put the pork in a roasting tin and roast 30 minutes. This will make sure the fat side crisps up properly. Reduce the oven temperature to 400°F [200°C] and roast another 2½ hours. Add the sherry to the tin 15 minutes before the end of the cooking time. Remove from the oven and leave to rest 10 minutes. Serve with the gravy in the bottom of the roasting tin, and something with a bit of acidity; a salad of fennel, radish, lemon juice, and a little oil makes a nice contrast.

COMFORT FOOD

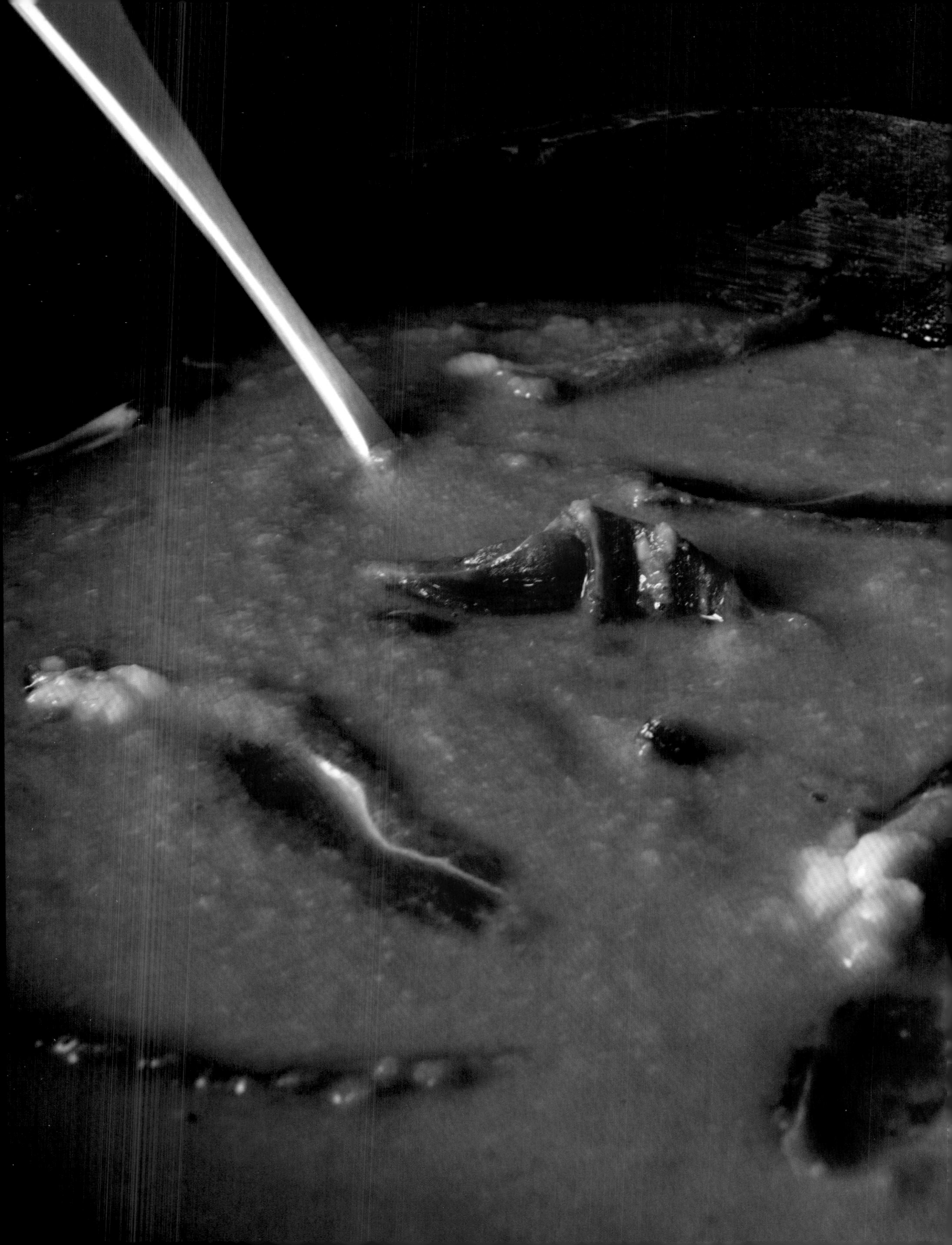

PEA & HAM HOCK SOUP

I love making this with smoked ham hock, which cuts through the sweetness of the peas beautifully. If you can't find it, use unsmoked or cured ham—any will do.

INGREDIENTS (SERVES 6)

1 x 1⅔ lb [750 g] smoked ham hock or knuckle
4½ cups [1 L] light chicken stock (see p. 245)
4 Tbsp butter
2 onions, diced
1 bay leaf
2 cloves
1⅛ lb [500 g] peas, freshly podded or frozen
Salt and black pepper

METHOD—Start by preparing the ham hock. Carefully carve the meat off the bone, reserving the bone. Shred the meat and set it aside—you're aiming for about 1¾ oz [50 g], or a small handful, per person.

Heat the chicken stock. Melt the butter in a large pan, add the onions and cook gently 4 to 5 minutes, or until softened.

Add the chicken stock, the reserved ham bone, bay leaf, and cloves. Bring to a boil and simmer 20 minutes. Add the peas and cook a further 10 minutes. Remove the bone, bay leaf, and cloves.

Transfer the soup to a blender, season with salt and pepper, and process until smooth. Pour into serving bowls, sprinkle the shredded ham over the top, and serve.

NEW ENGLAND CLAM CHOWDER

INGREDIENTS (SERVES 6)

40 fresh clams, such as American hard-shell or Amandes, or 12¼ oz [350 g] canned clams
4 Tbsp butter
3 bacon rashers, diced
1 onion, chopped
1 celery stalk, chopped
2 Tbsp flour
3 Tbsp dry white wine
2 cups [500 ml] fish or vegetable stock (see p. 248 to 249, or use water)
1 bay leaf
3 potatoes, cut into large dice
1 cup [250 ml] heavy cream
Salt and black pepper

METHOD—If using canned clams, drain them, keeping the liquid. If using fresh clams, clean them well and put them in a large pan with 2 Tbsp water. Cover and cook over high heat. As soon as they open, remove and shell them over a bowl to catch the liquid. Set aside.

Melt the butter in a heavy-based pan over low heat, add the bacon, and fry 4 to 5 minutes, or until crisp. Remove from the pan and set aside. Add the onion and soften 4 to 5 minutes, without letting them color. Add the celery and cook another 5 minutes, stirring occasionally, until translucent.

Increase the heat to medium, add the flour, and stir well. After 2 minutes, add the wine, stir well, and let it evaporate. Add the stock, the liquid from the clams, bay leaf, and potatoes. Bring to a boil, reduce the heat, and simmer, part-covered, about 20 minutes, or until tender. Finally, add the clams and cream and cook 5 minutes more. Season with salt and pepper. Serve with the crispy bacon sprinkled on top.

BOBOTIE

INGREDIENTS (SERVES 6)

2 slices medium white bread (or ½ cup breadcrumbs)

¾ cup [180 ml] milk

Butter, for greasing

2 Tbsp vegetable oil

2 onions, finely chopped

2 garlic cloves, crushed

½ tsp tamarind paste

2¼ lb [1 kg] ground beef

1 Tbsp brown sugar

Juice and grated zest of 1 lemon

⅓ cup [50 g] raisins

½ cup [50 g] slivered almonds, toasted

2 Tbsp mango chutney

1 egg

Salt and black pepper

TOPPING:

4 fresh bay leaves, lemon leaves, or kaffir lime leaves

1 egg

¼ cup [60 ml] milk

Salt

CAPE CURRY POWDER:

1 Tbsp cloves

2 Tbsp black peppercorns

3 Tbsp coriander seeds

3 Tbsp cumin seeds

1 Tbsp fennel seeds

1 Tbsp mustard seeds

2 small dried hot chilies (or 1 tsp chili flakes)

1 Tbsp cardamom seeds (shelled)

3 Tbsp fenugreek seeds

1 Tbsp turmeric

1 Tbsp ground ginger

This spicy cousin of meatloaf is a strong contender for the title of national dish of South Africa.

METHOD—Start by preparing the Cape curry powder. Lightly toast all the spices except the turmeric and ginger in a heavy-based pan. Using a spice mill or mortar and pestle, grind to a fine powder. Add the turmeric and ginger and mix well. Store in an airtight jar.

Preheat the oven to 325°F [170°C]. Soak the bread in the milk 10 minutes. Squeeze out, reserving the milk. Grease an approximately 9 in [22 cm] diameter baking dish with a little butter and set aside.

Heat the oil in a skillet, add the onions, and cook over low heat about 10 minutes, or until softened. Don't let them take on any color. Add the garlic, 3 Tbsp of the curry powder and tamarind, stir well, and cook 2 minutes more to release the flavors.

Put the meat in a large mixing bowl, add the spiced onions, sugar, lemon zest and juice, raisins, almonds, and chutney. Add the soaked, drained bread. Beat the reserved milk with 1 egg and stir it in, then season with salt and pepper. It should stick together well and come out of the bowl in one cohesive lump. Add a little more milk if the mixture is too dry. Transfer to the prepared dish. Use the bay or lime leaves to make a four-leaf clover pattern on top. Bake in the oven 35 minutes.

Mix the egg and milk for the topping and pour on top of the part-baked meatloaf, where it will form a pudding-like topping. Return to the oven for another 15 to 20 minutes, until set. Cover with aluminum foil if it gets too dark before it sets. Let cool a little before serving. Serve with rice and more chutney.

CHICKEN KIEV

A retro classic, and always a crowd pleaser. Beware the spurt of hot garlic butter when you dig in.

INGREDIENTS (SERVES 4)

⅔ cup [150 g] butter, softened

4 garlic cloves, crushed

1 Tbsp fresh flat-leaf parsley, chopped

1 Tbsp fresh tarragon, chopped

Juice of 1 lemon

4 chicken supremes (breasts with the trimmed bone still attached), skinned

2 eggs, lightly beaten

⅔ cup [80 g] flour

2½ cups [150 g] fine fresh breadcrumbs

Sunflower or vegetable oil, for frying

Salt and black pepper

METHOD—Combine the softened butter with the garlic, parsley, and tarragon. If you can't find fresh tarragon, just double the amount of parsley. Add a little lemon juice, season with salt and pepper, and combine well. Divide into 4 portions, form each one into a small sausage shape, wrap in plastic wrap, and flatten lightly. Set aside in the refrigerator.

Prepare the chicken breasts using a very sharp, small kitchen knife. Start by cutting off the thin mini-fillet from each breast and set aside. Make an incision along the side of the chicken breast, as deep into it as possible without piercing the opposite side, to create a pocket. Insert a chilled butter piece into each one and use the mini-fillet to plug the gap. You may have to trim it slightly to make it fit. Season the breast with salt and pepper on both sides.

Now set up your breadcrumbing station. Place the eggs, flour, and breadcrumbs in separate bowls. Working with one breast at a time, lightly dust it with flour, shaking off the excess, then dip in the egg mixture, before covering completely with breadcrumbs. Chill in the refrigerator 30 minutes until the coating is firm. Now repeat the process of coating—flour, beaten egg, breadcrumbs—and chill a further 30 minutes. This ensures a crispy crust and makes the precious garlic butter less likely to escape. Chill until ready to cook.

Preheat the oven to 400°F [200°C] and line a baking sheet with baking parchment. Heat a generous amount of oil—about 1 to 1½ in [3 to 4 cm] deep—in a large, high-sided skillet until very hot. Place the breaded chicken breasts carefully into the hot oil and fry 2 minutes on each side, or until golden. Remove with a slotted spoon and transfer to the prepared baking sheet. Bake in the oven 12 to 15 minutes, until the chicken is thoroughly cooked and the coating is crisp. Serve with rice.

MACARONI CARBONARA

Bacon, eggs, pasta, cheese: what's not to like? Macaroni works really well, but you can substitute other types of pasta. If you use more, or less, pasta, adjust the other ingredients accordingly, as the trick here is that the hot pasta effectively cooks the sauce. Too little pasta and you might end up with a cream soup, too much and you'll wonder where your sauce went.

INGREDIENTS (SERVES 4)

1 Tbsp olive oil

5 oz [140 g] pancetta, cut into matchstick-size pieces

4 egg yolks

⅓ cup [75 ml] heavy cream

1¼ cups [100 g] Parmesan cheese, grated

1⅔ cups [180 g] macaroni

Salt and black pepper

METHOD—Heat the olive oil in a large pan over low heat, add the pancetta, and cook gently 4 to 5 minutes, or until crisp.

Beat the egg yolks vigorously until they are a little frothy, then beat in the cream and season well with salt and pepper. Stir in half the Parmesan.

Bring a large pot of salted water to a boil, add the pasta, and cook according to the instructions on the packet. Drain and return to the pan. Stir the pancetta and oil into the pasta, then pour in the cream mixture. Stir to coat the pasta well. Add the remaining Parmesan and serve immediately.

FRENCH ONION SOUP

INGREDIENTS (SERVES 6)

7 Tbsp [100 g] butter

2¼ lb [1 kg] onions, thinly sliced

2 garlic cloves, finely chopped

Pinch of sugar

3¼ cups [750 ml] dry white wine

1 bay leaf

4½ cups [1 L] light veal or chicken stock
  (see p. 245–6), hot

1 baguette, cut into ¾ in [2 cm] slices

3 cups [250 g] Gruyère or Emmenthal cheese, grated

Salt and black pepper

METHOD—Melt the butter over low heat in a heavy-based pan and add the onions, garlic, and a pinch of sugar. Season with salt and pepper. Cook, stirring frequently, until they are completely soft and slightly browned. This should take about 35 minutes.

Increase the heat and add the wine and bay leaf. Once the liquid has reduced by half, add the hot stock, cover, and simmer 15 minutes, stirring occasionally. Preheat the grill and toast the baguette slices under the grill on both sides.

Place the soup in 6 heatproof serving bowls, add a piece of toast to each one, and generously cover with the grated cheese. Place under the grill for a few minutes, until the cheese is slightly browned, then serve immediately. Alternatively, place the toasts on a baking sheet, top with the cheese, and bake in the oven. Transfer to the serving bowls once the cheese has melted.

SHEPHERDS' PIE

This is delicious, simple comfort food. You can substitute beef for lamb, if you'd like a cottage pie instead.

INGREDIENTS (SERVES 6)

3 Tbsp vegetable oil

2¼ lb [1 kg] ground lamb

1 large onion, chopped

1 celery stalk, chopped

1 carrot, chopped

2 garlic cloves, crushed

2 Tbsp tomato paste

2 bay leaves

4 fresh thyme sprigs

2 cups [500 ml] hot lamb, chicken, or vegetable stock (see p. 245–9)

Salt and black pepper

MASH:

7 Tbsp [100 ml] milk

1 onion

1 bay leaf

2 cloves

6 black peppercorns

Pinch of grated nutmeg

2¼ lb [1 kg] mealy potatoes, such as Maris Piper, quartered

6 Tbsp [80 g] butter, plus extra for greasing

Salt and black pepper

METHOD—Start by preparing the milk for the mash. Heat it gently in a saucepan and add the onion, bay leaf, cloves, peppercorns, and nutmeg. Just before the milk comes to the boil, remove from the heat and leave to infuse at least 30 minutes.

Meanwhile, heat a little of the oil in a large pan over medium heat. When it is hot, add the ground meat in batches and cook, stirring, until browned. If the lamb is very fatty, carefully pour off most of the excess fat. Remove from the pan and set aside.

Add the remaining oil to the pan with the onion, celery, carrot, and garlic. Reduce the heat and let everything soften for 5 minutes, stirring occasionally. Add the tomato paste, stir well, and return the meat to the pan. Season with salt and pepper and add the thyme, bay leaf, and hot stock. Part-cover and simmer 45 minutes.

Preheat the oven to 400°F [200°C]. Bring a pan of salted water to a boil, add the potatoes, and cook 15 minutes, or until tender. Drain and return to the hot pan. Remove the spices from the milk and reheat it. Mash the potatoes with a potato ricer or masher, then add the flavored milk and butter; you need a fairly dry consistency. Season with salt and pepper.

Ladle the meat sauce into a large baking dish. Carefully spoon the mash on top, forming an even layer. Smooth it over and mark tracks all over it with a fork. Bake in the oven 20 minutes, or until the edges are bubbling and the surface is a pleasing golden brown.

PORK CHOPS
WITH APPLES & CELERY ROOT

INGREDIENTS (SERVES 4)

6 Tbsp [80 g] butter, plus extra for mashing

1 small head celery root, peeled and diced

4 large pork chops on the bone, about 1¼ in [3 cm] thick

2 fresh thyme sprigs, leaves picked

Olive oil, for frying

3 tart dessert apples, such as Cox or Braeburn, peeled and cut into wedges

Salt and black pepper

METHOD—Melt 4½ Tbsp [60 g] butter in a saucepan over medium heat. Add the celery root, season with salt and pepper, mix well, add a splash of water, cover, and cook 15 minutes, or until soft.

Using a sharp knife or scissors, score the fat on the edge of the pork chops. Season with salt and pepper and sprinkle with the thyme leaves.

Heat a little oil in a large skillet. When the pan is very hot, add the pork chops and brown well on both sides, then reduce the heat and cook about 5 minutes on each side, until the juices runs clear. They should be cooked through but still juicy, and the fat should be crispy. Remove from the skillet, cover with aluminum foil, and set aside to rest.

Put the apple wedges in the same pan and cook 4 minutes, until browned on both sides and slightly softened. Add a splash of water to the pan and stir to dissolve any sediment, then stir in the remaining butter.

Mash the celery root using a potato masher. Add a little more butter to taste and season with salt and pepper. Serve the chops with the mashed celery root, apples, and juices from the pan.

FISH & CHIPS

This is quintessential British comfort food.

INGREDIENTS (SERVES 4)

2½ cups [600 ml] sunflower or other neutral-flavored
   vegetable oil, plus 1 Tbsp

10½ oz [300 g] frozen peas

1 Tbsp fresh mint leaves, chopped

1 Tbsp butter

1 tsp lemon juice

1¾ lb [800 g] mealy potatoes, such as Maris Piper
   or King Edward

4 x 6½ oz [180 g] skinless cod or haddock fillets

1⅞ cups [225 g] self-rising flour, plus extra for dusting

1⅛ cups [280 ml] cold lager

1 quantity Tartare sauce (see p. 255)

Salt and black pepper

METHOD—First, prepare the peas. Heat 1 Tbsp oil in a saucepan and add the peas and mint. Cover and cook about 10 minutes, or until soft. Remove from the heat and mash the peas with a potato masher, or transfer to a food processor. Add the butter and lemon juice and season with salt and pepper. Set aside and keep warm.

Preheat the oven to 350°F [180°C] and line a baking dish with greaseproof paper. Heat the oil in the deep-fat fryer to 275°F [140°C].

Peel the potatoes and cut them into 2 in [5 cm] fries, or whatever size you prefer. Rinse well under cold water and pat dry thoroughly with a clean dish towel. Place them carefully into the hot oil and fry about 8 minutes (slightly less time for thin fries, longer if you have very large chunks). The potatoes should be soft and almost translucent in appearance, and should not take on any color. Remove them with a slotted spoon and place on paper towels to drain.

Increase the oil temperature to 375°F [190°C]. Prepare the batter by combining the sifted flour with a little salt and the lager. It should thinly coat the back of a wooden spoon; if it looks too thick, add a little more lager.

Season the fish fillets with salt and pepper and lightly dust them with flour. Shake off the excess. Dip the fillets into the batter so that they are fully coated and carefully transfer one at a time to the deep-fat fryer. Fry about 6 minutes, until the batter is golden and crisp. Remove with a slotted spoon, transfer to the prepared baking dish, and put in the oven to keep warm, until all the frying is completed.

Once the fish is cooked, return the cooled fries to the hot oil and fry another 3 minutes, until crisp and golden. Drain on paper towels, season with salt, and serve immediately along with the fish, peas, and tartare sauce.

GODFATHER SPAGHETTI
WITH MEATBALLS

"Heh, come over here, kid, learn something. You never know, you might have to cook for 20 guys some day. You see, you start out with a little bit of oil."

—Clemenza in *The Godfather* (1972)

A classic Italian-American dish immortalized on screen. The secret of good meatballs is bread. Italian immigrants to America originally added it to make the expensive meat go further, but it also ensures that they're light and giving.

INGREDIENTS (SERVES 6)

6½ oz [180 g] stale bread

14 Tbsp [200 ml] milk

1⅛ lb [500 g] ground meat (beef, a mixture of beef and veal, or a mixture of beef and pork)

3 garlic cloves, crushed

1 cup [80 g] pecorino or Parmesan cheese, grated

1 bunch fresh flat-leaf parsley, finely chopped

Finely grated zest of 1 lemon

3 eggs, beaten

14 Tbsp [200 ml] olive oil

1 tsp sugar

1 Tbsp tomato paste

7 Tbsp [100 ml] white wine

1¾ lb [800 g] canned tomatoes

Salt and black pepper

METHOD—Remove the crusts from the bread and cut into cubes. Soak in the milk 20 minutes, then squeeze out all the liquid. Place the ground meat, bread, 2 of the crushed garlic cloves, the grated cheese, parsley, lemon zest, and beaten eggs in a bowl, season with salt and pepper, and mix well with your hands.

Shape it into 20 balls about the size of a golf ball, or slightly larger. An ice-cream scoop might be of assistance here. Heat the oil in a large skillet. Be generous with the oil—it should be about ¼ in [5 mm] deep. When the oil is very hot, add a batch of meatballs and fry them until brown and crusty all over, which should take about 10 minutes. Remove with a slotted spoon and continue to fry the rest of them.

When all the meatballs have been fried, discard most of the oil, keeping back a little. Add the remaining crushed garlic clove and sugar to the pan and fry 1 minute. Add the tomato paste and heat through before adding the wine. Let the wine bubble 2 minutes, then add the tomatoes to the pan, breaking them up with a fork. Season with salt and pepper. Return the meatballs to the pan, then cover and simmer 25 minutes over medium heat, adding a little more liquid if necessary. Avoid stirring too much so that the meatballs don't break up. Serve with spaghetti.

GNOCCHI
WITH WALNUT SAUCE

Here the gnocchi are a foil to the flavor of the sauce. If possible, buy unshelled walnuts, as the preshelled ones are more likely to be old, and therefore potentially rancid.

INGREDIENTS (SERVES 4)

5 cups [500 g] walnuts (or 2 cups [200 g] unshelled)

3½ Tbsp [50 g] pine nuts

2 garlic cloves, chopped

2 Tbsp chopped fresh flat-leaf parsley

7 Tbsp [100 ml] olive oil

⅔ cup [50 g] Parmesan cheese, grated

Salt and black pepper

GNOCCHI:

1¼ cups [150 g] flour (Italian OO if you can get it),
  plus extra for dusting

8¾ oz [250 g] ricotta

3 egg yolks

2 Tbsp Parmesan cheese, grated

Salt and black pepper

METHOD—Start by preparing the sauce. If using unshelled walnuts, shell them: put them in a heatproof bowl and pour over boiling water to cover. Leave for a few minutes. Peel off the loosened skin. Depending on your nuts and your dexterity, this can be a little time consuming, but is well worth the effort.

Crush the walnuts lightly and toast them in a small pan over low heat, along with the pine nuts. No need to add any oil, as the nuts have enough of their own.

Use a mortar and pestle (or blender) to create a smooth paste with the nuts, garlic, and parsley, and season with salt and pepper. If you don't have a mortar and pestle, use a small food processor. Transfer to a bowl and add the olive oil, grated cheese, and 3 Tbsp water. Stir vigorously and set aside.

To make the gnocchi, first sift the flour into a bowl. Add the ricotta, egg yolks, and cheese, season with salt and pepper, and mix together to form a soft, wet dough.

Bring a large pan of generously salted water to a rolling boil so that it is ready as soon as all the gnocchi are prepared.

Flour your hands and work surface well and tip half the ricotta mixture onto it. Knead for 5 minutes. Roll the dough into a long thin sausage and cut into ¾ in [2 cm] dumplings. Repeat with the rest of the dough. If you are deft you can make them all in one batch.

Put your gnocchi in the boiling water. They are ready when all of then have bobbed to the surface, which should take 2 to 4 minutes. Remove carefully with a slotted spoon, place in serving plates, and spoon over the sauce. Serve immediately.

WIENER SCHNITZEL
WITH POTATO SALAD

Veritably waltzes down your throat.

INGREDIENTS (SERVES 4)

4 veal escalopes

2 Tbsp flour

⅞ cup [100 g] fine, fresh breadcrumbs

2 eggs, lightly beaten

⅔ cup [150 g] clarified butter

3½ Tbsp groundnut oil

½ bunch fresh flat-leaf parsley

8 lemon wedges

Salt and white pepper

POTATO SALAD:

1¾ lb [800 g] boiling potatoes, unpeeled

3 Tbsp white wine vinegar

1 Tbsp lemon juice

1 tsp sugar

1 Tbsp mustard (optional)

2 shallots, finely chopped

⅝ cup [150 ml] stock, such as vegetable,
   beef, or chicken, hot

1 bunch radishes or gherkins, thinly sliced

4 Tbsp sunflower oil

1 bunch fresh chives, chopped

Salt and black pepper

METHOD—Start by making the potato salad. Bring a large pan of salted water to a boil, add the potatoes and cook 10 to 15 minutes, or until tender. Combine the vinegar, lemon juice, sugar, mustard, and shallots in a bowl and season with salt and pepper. Drain the potatoes, then peel and slice them while still warm, add them to the onion mixture, and pour over the hot stock. Add the sliced radishes or gherkins and the sunflower oil and leave to macerate for 20 minutes. Stir in the chives just before serving. Do not make the salad too far in advance.

Rub the escalopes with damp paper towels, cover with plastic wrap, and flatten the meat lightly with a rolling pin. They should be very thin—about ⅛ in [3 mm] thick. Season with salt and a little white pepper on both sides. Place the flour, breadcrumbs, and eggs on separate plates. Meanwhile, heat the clarified butter and groundnut oil in a large skillet until very hot. You need enough fat for the meat to swim. Dip the escalopes in the flour on both sides and shake off the excess, then dip in the egg mixture, and finally into the breadcrumbs to coat. Add them to the hot pan immediately and cook on both sides 1 to 2 minutes on each side, until golden brown in color.

During frying, tilt the pan occasionally so that the oil covers most of the breaded surface and it swells up. Remove from the pan and place on paper towels to drain off the excess fat. Sprinkle with parsley and serve immediately with the lemon wedges and potato salad.

MUSSELS IN BEER

A steaming plate of mussels is a welcome sight indeed. Dispatch with gusto.

INGREDIENTS (SERVES 6)

9 lb [4 kg] mussels

4 Tbsp butter

2 shallots, diced

2 celery stalks, diced

2 cups [500 ml] wheat beer

Juice of ½ lemon

1 bunch fresh flat-leaf parsley, chopped

Black pepper

METHOD—Wash and scrub the mussels thoroughly in several changes of cold water. Pull off and discard the beards (the strings hanging out of the shell). Discard any open mussels that do not close when firmly tapped on the shell, or any that feel very heavy.

Melt the butter in a large casserole dish and add the shallots and celery. Cook 2 to 3 minutes, or until slightly softened, then add the beer and lemon juice. Season with pepper and bring to a boil. Cook 5 minutes, then add the mussels and cover. Cook another 5 minutes, occasionally shaking the pan.

Remove any mussels that have not opened, add the chopped parsley, and serve at once with the cooking liquid and white bread, or Belgian-style, with fries.

WHOLE ROAST SUCKLING PIG

Nothing says "feast" more than a whole roast suckling pig (with an apple in its mouth, naturally). Remember to order a piglet from your butcher that fits into your oven—most domestic ovens won't accommodate a beast heavier than 20 lb [9 kg].

INGREDIENTS (SERVES 10)

1 whole suckling pig, about 15 lb [7 kg]
3 lb [1.5 kg] salt
3¾ cups [750 g] sugar
1 apple
7 Tbsp [100 ml] olive oil
Salt and black pepper

METHOD—First, wash the pig under cold running water. Put it in a large container or bucket and add the salt, sugar, and 10½ qt [10 L] water. Leave it in the brine at least 12 hours, turning it once.

Preheat the oven to 350°F [180°C]. Remove the pig from the brine and pat it dry thoroughly with paper towels. Stuff it with crumpled aluminum foil to help support it during roasting.

Transfer it to a roasting rack with an oven tray underneath, with the hind legs tucked under the belly and the front legs pointing forward along the sides. Put an apple in its mouth. Prop the head up with some foil underneath it. Rub the pig all over with olive oil and season generously with salt and pepper. Put some foil over each ear; remove this foil after 2 hours.

Roast the pig about 3 to 3½ hours. Your pig is cooked when the juices run clear and the skin is crisp and dark amber in color.

Remove from the oven, let rest 20 minutes, remove the foil from the cavity, and carve. Serve with steamed potatoes and spring vegetables.

PEPPERED STEAK

INGREDIENTS (SERVES 4)

4 fillet, rump, or sirloin steaks, about 8 oz [225 g] each
   and 1¼ in [3 cm] thick

2 Tbsp neutral-flavored oil

Crushed black peppercorns, to taste

4 Tbsp butter, chilled and diced

½ cup [120 ml] dry white wine

7 Tbsp [100 ml] good-quality dark veal stock
   or demi-glace (see p. 249, or buy it at the
   butcher or deli)

1 Tbsp heavy cream (optional)

1 Tbsp Dijon mustard (optional)

Salt

Peppered steak is very Zen. It's all about the balance between steak, pepper, and sauce. Even if you don't reach perfection, you'll have a great time trying. It makes a quick, easy supper, but would be just as at home at a dinner party. It's important to use a lean, not too fatty cut here.

METHOD—Preheat the oven to 250°F [120°C] and put a serving dish in to warm.

Brush the steaks with a little of the oil and dredge them in the crushed peppercorns. Push the peppercorns down well so that they stick. Season well with salt all over.

Heat the remaining oil in a skillet, and add a couple of pieces of butter once it is hot. When the butter foams, add the steaks, cook about 5 minutes on each side for medium, and transfer to the warmed serving dish. Cover with aluminum foil.

Pour the white wine into the pan and bring to a boil. Stir well, scraping the bottom of the pan to dissolve any sediment, and reduce by half. Add the stock and reduce over medium heat until the sauce becomes syrupy. Stir in the remaining chilled, diced butter. If you want a creamy sauce, add the cream now. If you want the mustard too, stir it in at this point. Transfer the steaks to plates and pour over the unctuous sauce. Serve immediately with sautéed potatoes or fries (see p. 104).

CHOUCROUTE GARNIE

If you like pork, you'll love this dish. Every aspect of the pig is celebrated in it. I've been precise about the ingredients listed below, but you can see what meats are available at your butcher and improvise with a mixture of cured, raw, and smoked pork. This dish is exceptionally forgiving, and it's quite hard to make something that isn't delicious.

INGREDIENTS (SERVES 8)

4½ lb [2 kg] Sauerkraut, washed (see p. 212)

1 raw ham hock or knuckle, about 1¾ lb [800 g]

1½ lb [700 g] smoked pork shoulder

1⅛ lb [500 g] salted pork belly

6 Tbsp [80 g] duck or goose fat

2 onions, chopped

3¼ cups [750 ml] off-dry white wine, such as Riesling

1 Tbsp juniper berries

1 tsp black peppercorns

2 bay leaves

2 cloves

2 garlic cloves

8 small chipolatas

8 Strasbourg sausages or frankfurters

METHOD—Preheat the oven to 350°F [180°C]. Wash the sauerkraut thoroughly in cold water until the water runs clear. Squeeze out the liquid completely with your hands.

Put the meats, except the sausages, in a large pot and cover with water. Bring to a boil and cook 5 minutes. Drain.

In a large casserole dish, heat the duck or goose fat and fry the onions over low heat 5 minutes, or until softened. Add the sauerkraut and stir. Add the wine, spices, and garlic cloves, and tuck in the ham hock and pork shoulder. Pour over 2 cups [500 ml] hot water, cover and bring to a simmer. Put in the oven and cook 1 hour.

Remove from the oven, add the pork belly, and return to the oven a further 2 hours. Check that there is enough liquid at the bottom and top up with hot water if necessary. Thirty minutes before the end of cooking, add the chipolatas to the casserole.

Twenty minutes before the end of cooking, bring a large pan of water to a boil and add the Strasbourg sausages. Simmer 3 minutes, or until heated through. Remove and transfer them to the casserole in the oven and cook a further 10 minutes.

Remove the casserole from the oven and remove the bay leaves, cloves, garlic cloves, and as many juniper berries and peppercorns as you can catch. Remove and slice the meat. Serve the choucroute on a large serving platter with the sliced meat and the sausages on top, with steamed potatoes on the side.

ROAST BONE MARROW

This is perfect spread on toast with a pinch of salt and a few pickles on the side. It's also good with a big pinch of gremolata. A hot watercress or arugula salad, or a bitter endive or radicchio salad, sharply dressed, would work nicely too.

INGREDIENTS (SERVES 4)

5 x 3 in [12 x 8 cm] pieces veal marrow bone, about 4½ lb [2 kg]
4 slices of toasted white bread
1 quantity Gremolata (see p. 148)
Salt and black pepper

METHOD—Preheat the oven to 475°F [240°C]. Put your marrow bones on a roasting tray and roast 20 to 25 minutes, or until the edges are a bit scorched and the marrow has become loose. While they are in the oven, make the gremolata, if using, and prepare a stack of toast. Remove the bones from the oven. Serve with a tsp to scoop out the marrow onto the toast.

POT AU FEU

INGREDIENTS (SERVES 8)

4½ lb [2 kg] mixed cuts of beef on the bone, such as shoulder, knuckle, silverside, oxtail
3 turnips, quartered
2 carrots, halved
2 onions, quartered with the root on
2 celery stalks, cut into 4 pieces
2 garlic cloves
1 bouquet garni
15 black peppercorns
3 cloves
3 leeks, white parts only, halved
4 potatoes, halved
Salt and black pepper

There is nothing more satisfying on a cold winter's night than this classic meat-and-broth dish.

METHOD—Put the beef in a large casserole dish and cover with cold water. Season with salt. Put over low heat, bring to a boil gently, and simmer 2 minutes. Skim several times.

Add the turnips, carrots, onions, celery, garlic, bouquet garni, peppercorns, and cloves and simmer gently 1½ hours. Skim off the fat. Add the leeks and potatoes and cook another hour.

Remove the bouquet garni and cloves and season with salt and pepper. Serve with mustard, pickled gherkins, and fresh bread.

BRITISH BEEF CARPACCIO

This is my butch version of the classic Italian dish. The original was famously created in Harry's Bar in Venice from what they had available. Happily, they had some gorgeous raw beef to hand—but unfortunately they also had mayonnaise and Worcestershire sauce. To me, it's far better to put the beef center stage. In this recipe, the beef is charred briefly but remains essentially, deliciously raw. The watercress and mustard give it a bit of pep.

INGREDIENTS (SERVES 4)

1⅛ lb [500 g] beef fillet

1 Tbsp olive oil, plus extra for cooking

1 tsp red wine vinegar

½ tsp English mustard

7 oz [200 g] watercress

1 shallot, finely sliced

Salt and coarsely ground black pepper

METHOD—Try to get fillet cut from the thinner tail end; it will have a better shape. Trim any fat, nerves, or gristle off the fillet.

Make an iced water bath in a bowl large enough to hold your fillet comfortably. Heat a ridged grill pan until it is very hot.

Brush the meat all over with olive oil and rub with salt and pepper. Put the fillet on the grill pan and char 1 minute on each side (4 minutes in total). Put the meat in the iced water briefly to stop it cooking. Pat the meat dry with paper towels and set aside.

When ready to serve, combine the olive oil, vinegar, and mustard in a bowl, season with salt and pepper, and toss the watercress and shallot in the mixture.

Carve the beef into thin slices with a very sharp knife at an angle of about 30°. Arrange the sliced beef on top of the salad and serve.

COTECHINO
WITH LENTILS

This heavyweight pork-and-lentil dish is a meal in itself, but you can also serve it with polenta as the Italians do, or simply with mash. Don't underestimate how filling it is, though. Mostarda di Cremona (preserved fruits with mustard), with their sweet, hot punch, are great with it.

INGREDIENTS (SERVES 4)

1⅓ lb [600 g] cotechino or zampone sausage (available at Italian delis)

12¼ oz [350 g] green lentils

2 onions, 1 finely chopped

1 carrot

1 bay leaf

6 black peppercorns

Oil, for frying

1 celery stalk, chopped

¼ cup [50 g] pancetta, finely chopped

Salt and black pepper

METHOD—Pierce the skin of the sausage all over with a needle and wrap it tightly in muslin (some sausages are sold in a special plastic wrapper that can be used for the cooking). Put in a casserole dish that will hold the sausage snugly and cover with cold water. Bring the liquid slowly to a boil over low heat and simmer about 2 hours.

Meanwhile, put the lentils in a saucepan with the whole onion, carrot, bay leaf, peppercorns, and salt. Add water and cook about 45 minutes, or until tender. Remove the onion, carrot, bay leaf, and peppercorns, and drain the lentils.

Heat a little oil in a pan, add the chopped onion, celery, and pancetta and cook 2 minutes. Add the lentils, stir well, and season with salt and pepper. Add 2 ladles of the cotechino cooking liquid. Cover and simmer over low heat, stirring occasionally, until the liquid has been completely absorbed—about 15 minutes.

Remove the sausage from the casserole, discard the wrapping and slice it into ⅜ in [1 cm] rounds. Put the lentils on a serving platter with the sausage slices on top.

STUFFED PIG'S TROTTER

This is the signature dish of legendary chef Pierre Koffman. Unlike much of haute cuisine, it is relatively easy to prepare at home—the only tricky bit is deboning the trotters (see p. 272). The sweetbreads can be replaced with more chicken, and the morels with less grand mushrooms.

INGREDIENTS (SERVES 4)

4 pigs' back trotters, boned
  (see p. 272)
3½ oz [100 g] carrots, finely chopped
3½ oz [100 g] onions, finely chopped
⅝ cup [150 ml] dry white wine
1 Tbsp port
⅝ cup [150 ml] veal stock (see p. 249)
8 oz [225 g] veal sweetbreads
5 Tbsp [75 g] butter, plus 4 tsp for the sauce
20 dried morels, soaked and drained
1 small onion, finely chopped
1 chicken breast, skinned and diced
1 egg white
14 Tbsp [200 ml] heavy cream
Salt and black pepper

METHOD—Preheat the oven to 325°F [160°C]. Put the trotters in a casserole dish with the carrots and onions, the wine, port, and veal stock. Cover and braise in the oven 3 hours.

Bring a pan of water to a simmer, add the sweetbreads, and blanch 30 seconds, then remove and put in a bowl of iced water. Remove after 1 minute, then pat dry with a clean dish towel. Chop them, then fry in the butter 5 minutes, add the morels and chopped onion, and cook another 5 minutes. Let cool. Purée the chicken breast in a food processor with the egg white and cream, and season with salt and pepper. Mix with the sweetbreads and morels to make the stuffing. Take the trotters out of the casserole and strain the cooking stock, reserving the stock but discarding the vegetables. Open the trotters out flat and lay each one on a piece of foil. Let cool, then fill the cooled trotters with the stuffing and roll tightly in foil to make a nice shape, tying the ends. Chill in the refrigerator at least 2 hours.

Prepare a steamer and steam the foil-wrapped trotters until heated through. Alternatively, preheat the oven to 425°F [220°C], and cook in the oven, covered, 15 minutes. Pour the reserved stock into a pan and reduce by half. Whisk in a knob of butter, pour the sauce over the trotters, and serve very hot, with buttery mash.

STEAK TARTARE

This dish tends to cause a fight-or-flight response in diners. Some people can be unsettled just by reading "spiced raw beef topped with a raw egg yolk," while others dive in. It's worth tasting if you've never tried it; it's easy to make and utterly delicious. The Tartars made this dish with horsemeat; although I never say never, I find it hard to imagine that this could be as good as beef fillet. I have suggested a classic combination of additions, but you can alter it as you like. Indeed, it is often served with little dishes of the accompaniments so that diners can make their own individually spiced tartare.

INGREDIENTS (SERVES 4)

1½ lb [700 g] fillet steak, or other lean beef cut

2 tsp Dijon mustard

4 Tbsp groundnut or other neutral-flavored oil

4 Tbsp finely chopped white onion

4 tsp capers, chopped

2 tsp fresh flat-leaf parsley, finely chopped

1 Tbsp ketchup (optional)

Worcestershire sauce, to taste

Tabasco sauce, to taste

4 egg yolks, the freshest you can find

Salt and black pepper

METHOD—Chop the meat finely with a sharp knife, first shredding the steak, then chopping across the strands, and repeat, changing the angle of the knife to the meat each time.

Put the mustard in a bowl large enough to incorporate all the ingredients and add the oil, beating slowly with a fork. Add the onion, capers, parsley, ketchup, Worcestershire, and Tabasco sauces. Combine gently but thoroughly.

Now add the meat to the sauce, season with salt and pepper, and mix together with a fork until you have an even consistency.

Divide the meat into 4 equal portions and shape into rough rounds. Using your thumb, make a dip in the top of each pile and carefully spoon an egg yolk into each dip, taking care not to break it. Serve immediately.

BEEF STEAK FLORENTINE STYLE

INGREDIENTS (SERVES 2)

2 x 1½ in [4 cm] thick T-bone steaks,
   about 1⅓ lb [600 g] each

Olive oil, for cooking

1 lemon, cut into wedges

Salt and black pepper

"Burn me a good thick one . . . meat and potatoes!"

—John Wayne in *The Man Who Shot Liberty Valance* (1962)

METHOD—Pat the steaks dry with paper towels on both sides and bring them to room temperature. Do not season or flatten them. Light the barbecue, using wood if possible.

When the wood on your barbecue has become glowing embers (or, if using charcoal, when the coals are white), put the meat, unseasoned, on the grill and cook 5 minutes on each side to cook it to the classic rare. When you turn the steak over, season it with salt and pepper on the browned side. Season the other side when it has cooked. Turn it over one last time to shake off any excess salt.

Remove from the grill, put on a large platter, drizzle a few drops of olive oil over, and serve with lemon wedges.

HEALTHY

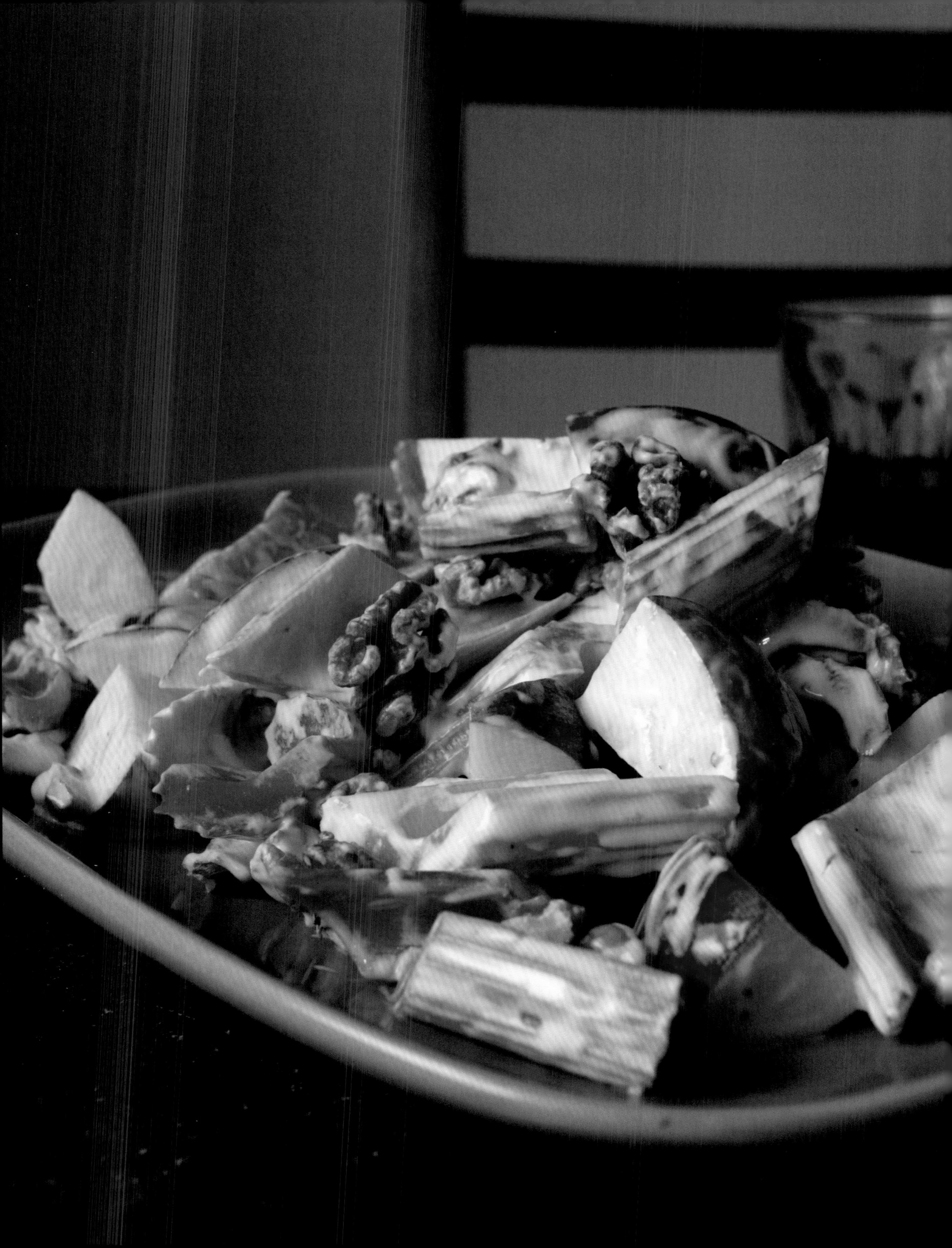

WALDORF SALAD

INGREDIENTS (SERVES 2)

⅓ cup [40 g] walnuts, chopped
1 Tbsp lemon juice, freshly squeezed
2 celery stalks, sliced into small chunks
1 apple, cored and sliced into wedges
4 Tbsp natural yogurt
Salt and black pepper

Good as an appetizer or a light lunch. If you need something more substantial, have a grilled chicken breast on the side.

METHOD—Heat a skillet over low heat and add the walnuts. Toast them lightly for a few minutes, shaking the pan occasionally and making sure they don't burn. Tip them out of the pan when ready.

Mix together the yogurt and lemon juice and season with salt and pepper. Add the walnuts, celery, and apple pieces and stir to coat well.

MEXICAN CEVICHE SHRIMP COCKTAIL

Ceviche, which is basically raw seafood that has been cured or "cooked" in lime juice, is popular all over Central and South America. In Peru it is the national dish. This Mexican version, a delicious rough salsa and shrimp concoction, is more exuberant—a kind of Latin shrimp salad. Always use the very freshest seafood; if you can't find any, make something else.

INGREDIENTS (SERVES 4)

1⅛ lb [500 g] very fresh raw tiger shrimps, shelled
7 limes
3 garlic cloves, finely chopped
2 large red onions, very thinly sliced
2 ripe avocados, sliced and diced
6 tomatoes, sliced and diced
2 large red mild chilies, finely chopped
10 fresh cilantro sprigs
Salt

METHOD—If you are using large shrimp you might want to devein them—that is, remove the gray-black vein that runs lengthwise down the back of the shrimp—although I've never seen anyone do this in Mexico. It's quite tricky: using a small, sharp knife, make a slit along the back and lift out the dark, stringy vein. Rinse them and pat them dry with paper towels. Set aside in a cool place.

Next, juice the limes. It helps to roll them under your palm, applying a little pressure, before squeezing them. Cut them in half and squeeze them firmly, but don't crush them or the juice may become bitter.

Put the shrimp and lime juice in a bowl with a pinch of salt. Cover and chill in the refrigerator 2 hours. Toss the shrimp in the lime and salt every now and again.

After 2 hours, crush the garlic to a paste with some salt and the back of a knife. Add the garlic, red onions, avocados, tomatoes, and chilies to the shrimp and lime mixture, stir well, and return to the refrigerator for another 30 minutes.

Chop the cilantro, stir it in, and serve immediately. Mexicans are fond of serving this in individual glass bowls—the kind you serve ice cream or shrimp salad in. Ceviche is also good with nachos (see p. 48).

JEWISH PENICILLIN

A.K.A. chicken noodle soup with matzo balls. Classic.

INGREDIENTS (SERVES 6)

2 carrots, diced

1 onion, diced

2 celery stalks, sliced

1 leek, white part only, sliced

1 x 4½ lb [2 kg] chicken,
  preferably an old boiling fowl with giblets

1 handful egg noodles

1 Tbsp fresh flat-leaf parsley, chopped

Salt and black pepper

MATZO BALLS:

2 Tbsp vegetable oil (if needed)

1 egg

3 oz [80 g] matzo meal

2 Tbsp chicken broth or stock

¼ tsp grated nutmeg

Salt and black pepper

METHOD—Place the carrots, onion, celery, and leek in a large pan with the chicken giblets (don't use the liver). Fill the pot with about 2 qt [2 L] water, place over medium heat, and bring to a rolling boil. After a few minutes, reduce the heat and remove the scum from the surface with a slotted spoon. Scoop off the chicken fat from the surface and reserve it to use in the matzo balls. Cover and cook 2½ hours (if using a boiling fowl; if using an ordinary chicken, remove it after 1 hour, remove the meat from the carcass and return the bones to the pot). If there is a lot less liquid at the end, top up with more water.

Remove the chicken or carcass and the giblets. If you prefer a crystal-clear soup, strain the broth through a fine sieve lined with muslin. Remove as much fat as you like (this is easiest when the broth has cooled down completely) and set aside.

For the matzo balls, whisk together 2 Tbsp of the reserved chicken fat (if you don't have enough, use vegetable oil), egg, matzo meal, and broth or stock. Add the nutmeg and season with salt and pepper. Cover and leave to rest in the refrigerator for at least 2 hours, or until chilled.

Bring a large pan of salted water to a gentle simmer. With moist hands, shape the matzo mixture into dumplings the size of table tennis balls and add them to the pan. Simmer 1 hour.

When almost ready to serve, heat the chicken soup and add a handful of egg noodles to it. Simmer about 5 minutes (or according to the instructions on the packet). Add the boiled matzo balls and chopped parsley. If you used a boiling fowl, you may have a lot of fat on the surface. Skim some of it away, but don't remove all of it—it is part of the dish.

Traditionally, the broth and matzo balls are served first and the chicken afterward, perhaps with a few pickles.

MACKEREL, BEET & HORSERADISH SALAD

This is a punchy salad with a full-on flavor.

INGREDIENTS (SERVES 2)
SALAD:

1 fresh mackerel

Olive oil, for cooking

8¾ oz [250 g] boiled new potatoes

2 large, cooked beets, peeled

2 good handfuls of salad leaves of choice (preferably including arugula or watercress)

2 fresh dill sprigs, chopped (optional)

1 celery stalk, thinly sliced

1 Tbsp roughly chopped walnuts

Salt and black pepper

DRESSING:

1 tsp wholegrain mustard

1 tsp honey

1 Tbsp cider vinegar

1 to 2 tsp creamed horseradish, or to taste

4 Tbsp olive oil

Salt and black pepper

METHOD—Brush the mackerel with olive oil. Heat a ridged grill pan or skillet until it is very hot, add the mackerel, and cook 4 minutes on each side, turning once. When the mackerel has cooled just enough to handle, carefully make an incision along the head on one side until you reach the bone. Then cut along the back of the fish, sliding the blade toward the tail. Push the tip of your knife or fish slice under the fillet and carefully lift it off the bone. Pick up the tail and lift the bone and the head clean away from the fillet lying underneath.

To make the dressing, whisk together the mustard, honey, water, vinegar, and horseradish with 2 tsp water. Season with salt and pepper. When amalgamated, add the oil and combine well.

Cut the potatoes and beets into bite-size pieces. Season with salt and pepper. Put the salad leaves, dill (if using), celery, and walnuts in a bowl and toss with some of the dressing. Dress the potatoes and beets separately. Do not overmix them—purple food does not look good! Assemble the two salads and the fish and serve.

GRILLED WILD SALMON
WITH WILTED GREENS

Wild salmon bears little relation to the comparatively dreary farmed variety. That this might come as news to anyone shows just how far wrong we have gone. It is packed with flavor, and since it swam in the sea throughout its life, it is altogether meatier for it. It looks like salmon ought to: dark orange. Along with the spinach, it is a really simple, healthy, tasty, and filling meal. Serve with red rice, if you like.

INGREDIENTS (SERVES 4)

4 wild salmon steaks

Olive oil, for cooking

1⅔ lb [750 g] fresh baby spinach, washed and dried

1 lemon, cut into wedges

Salt and black pepper

METHOD—Preheat a flat griddle pan or large skillet until it is very hot. Whatever you use, you need a flat, not a ridged surface. Brush the salmon steaks all over with olive oil. Season the skin side with salt. Place skin-side down on the pan and cook 4 minutes. The skin should be well charred. Turn and cook 2 minutes on the other side. Remove from the grill and set aside to rest.

When you turn the fish, add the spinach to another part of the pan with a drizzle of olive oil, or cook it in a separate pan. It will cook very quickly, so turn it rapidly and frequently for about 2 minutes. It is ready when it is visibly cooked through and wilted. Dress it with a squeeze of lemon and season with salt and pepper. At home, I eat this dish with more lemon slices, a light chili sauce, black olive paste, or a dollop of garlic mayonnaise.

HEARTY MINESTRONE

INGREDIENTS (SERVES 6)

10½ oz [300 g] canned cannellini beans

3 Tbsp olive oil, plus extra for drizzling

1 large onion, diced

2 garlic cloves, sliced

2 celery stalks, diced

2 carrots, sliced

1¾ oz [50 g] pancetta, diced

2 tomatoes, skinned, seeded, and chopped

2 zucchini, trimmed and sliced

2 potatoes, diced

1 Tbsp fresh flat-leaf parsley, leaves chopped

1 Savoy cabbage, shredded

3½ oz [100 g] rice or soup noodles

10 fresh basil leaves, torn

Salt and black pepper

Grated Parmesan cheese, to serve

METHOD—Drain the beans, rinse them, and drain again. In a large casserole, heat the olive oil and add the onion, garlic, celery, carrot, and pancetta. Cook 5 minutes, then add all the vegetables except the cabbage. Add enough water to cover the ingredients. Season with salt and pepper and simmer 3 hours.

Add the shredded cabbage and simmer another 20 minutes before adding the rice or soup noodles. Cook another 15 minutes, or check the instructions on the packet. Add the basil leaves and a drizzle of olive oil. Serve with grated Parmesan to sprinkle over.

SOM TAM SALAD

This spicy green papaya salad is ubiquitous in Thailand and it is quite addictive, so although the recipe states that it serves four, this depends entirely on how greedy you are.

INGREDIENTS (SERVES 4)

6 garlic cloves

1 tsp salt

3 bird's eye chilies

1 Tbsp dried shrimp

1 handful dry-roasted peanuts

Juice of 1 lime

1 large, green papaya (or a green mango), peeled and sliced into matchsticks

3½ oz [100 g] trimmed French beans, cut in half

10 cherry or baby plum tomatoes, quartered

1 Tbsp palm or brown sugar

1 Tbsp fish sauce

METHOD—Pound the garlic, salt, and chilies into a rough paste using a large mortar and pestle. Add the shrimp, peanuts, and a good squeeze of lime juice and pound again. Set aside.

Add the papaya, French beans, and tomatoes and bruise gently so the paste gets worked into them, but not so much that you pulp the fruit. Don't worry if your mortar is not big enough to hold all the papaya and beans; just make sure you pound at least some of each with the paste.

Tip everything out of the mortar into a large bowl. Add the rest of the papaya, tomatoes, and beans if you did not pound them in the mortar.

Add the sugar, fish sauce, and the rest of the juice from the lime and stir thoroughly. Serve immediately.

TANDOORI CHICKEN

INGREDIENTS (SERVES 6)

6 chicken legs

2 tsp chili powder (preferably Kashmiri)

1 Tbsp lime juice

⅓ cup [80 ml] thick natural yogurt

1 tsp ground coriander

1 tsp ground cumin

1 tsp garam masala

1 Tbsp fresh ginger paste

4 garlic cloves, crushed

½ tsp saffron threads

1 tsp dried fenugreek leaves

½ tsp ground black pepper

2 Tbsp vegetable oil

2 Tbsp lemon juice

1 quantity Naan bread (see p. 263), to serve

Salt

RAITA:

1⅔ cup [400 ml] natural yogurt

1 cucumber, grated

½ tsp cumin seeds, toasted and crushed

Juice of ½ lemon

Salt and black pepper

METHOD—Using a sharp knife, slash the chicken legs 3 or 4 times. Mix half the chili powder with the lime juice, sprinkle over the legs, and season with salt. Set aside for 20 minutes.

Meanwhile, make your marinade. First, put the yogurt in the middle of a muslin cloth and tie it tightly, attach it to a long wooden spoon and leave to hang over a bowl to catch the drips for 20 minutes.

Once the yogurt has drained, put it in a bowl with the coriander, cumin, garam masala, ginger, garlic, remaining chili powder, saffron, fenugreek leaves, pepper, oil, lemon juice, and salt. Stir well and rub over the chicken legs, forcing the marinade well into the slits. Put in a bowl, cover with plastic wrap, and leave to marinate 4 hours in the refrigerator.

Preheat the oven to 475°F [240°C]. Put the chicken on a baking sheet and cook in the oven 20 minutes, or until tender. Meanwhile, prepare the raita: combine the yogurt and cucumber in a mixing bowl. Season with cumin, salt, pepper, and lemon juice. Remove and serve with lemon wedges, sliced onions, raita, and naan.

CHICKEN TAGINE

WITH PRESERVED LEMONS & OLIVES

INGREDIENTS (SERVES 4)

4 Tbsp olive oil

2 onions, chopped

2 garlic cloves, chopped

1 fresh red chili, finely chopped

1 tsp ground cumin

1 tsp ground ginger

½ tsp ground cinnamon

½ tsp ras el hanout (optional)

1 x 3 lb [1.5 kg] chicken, jointed into 10 pieces

6 small or 3 large preserved lemons (see p. 207)

½ tsp saffron threads

1 cup [250 ml] chicken stock (see p. 245)

3½ oz [100 g] green olives

4 tsp fresh cilantro leaves, chopped

Salt and black pepper

METHOD—Heat the olive oil in a tagine or large casserole dish and cook the onions 5 minutes, or until soft. Add the garlic and chili and cook for a further minute. Now add the spices and cook 2 to 3 minutes, until aromatic. Add the chicken pieces and coat well in the spice-onion mixture. Chop the preserved lemons and add them to the pan along with the saffron and stock. Bring to a gentle simmer and cook, covered, 1 hour.

Add the olives and cook another 15 minutes. Sprinkle with chopped cilantro and serve with couscous.

IMAM BAYILDI

Literally "the Imam fainted." As for why, no-one knows for sure, but whatever the reason, it is an utterly delicious dish that, for once, is not improved by the addition of meat.

INGREDIENTS (SERVES 4)

4 medium-sized eggplants
Olive oil, for frying
2 onions, chopped
6 garlic cloves, chopped
2 tsp sugar
1 Tbsp lemon juice
6 ripe tomatoes, chopped
1 Tbsp fresh flat-leaf parsley, chopped
Salt and black pepper

METHOD—Wash and dry the eggplants. Lightly score their skin lengthwise about ¾ in [2 cm] apart with a knife and peel off strips, creating an alternating black-and-white pattern. Cut in half lengthwise, keeping the stalk on. Cut 3 incisions lengthwise into the flesh of the eggplant, being careful not to cut all the way through. Salt generously and place flesh-side down on a plate. After 30 minutes, wash the salt off and pat dry with paper towels.

Preheat the oven to 375°F [190°C]. Heat some of the olive oil in a large skillet. Fry the eggplants until lightly browned all over, about 3 minutes on each side. Don't overcook them—they will still be raw in the middle. Remove from the pan and set aside.

Add a little more oil to the pan and cook the onions and garlic over low heat about 5 minutes, until soft. Add the sugar, lemon juice, chopped tomatoes, and parsley and season with salt and pepper. Cook 2 minutes, or until thickened.

Place the eggplants in a gratin dish or shallow baking sheet and spoon the tomato sauce over, pressing it deeply into the incisions. Add 3 Tbsp water and drizzle a little oil on top, cover with aluminum foil, and bake in the oven 1 hour.

Remove from the oven and let cool slightly before serving with white bread and Greek yogurt.

TUNA & SALMON SASHIMI

INGREDIENTS (SERVES 4)

14 oz [400 g] very fresh tuna fillet, chilled

14 oz [400 g] very fresh salmon fillet, skinned and chilled

1 tsp wasabi paste

4 Tbsp soy sauce

You don't need to train for decades to make good sashimi at home. As long as you use the freshest fish available, it will be a treat. Use large fish fillets, as they are easier to prepare, and only buy fish for sashimi from a trusted fishmonger. You are eating raw fish, after all.

METHOD—First, prepare the fish. Using a sharp knife, trim each one to get a nice, clean rectangle about 1½ in [4 cm] wide and ¾ in [2 cm] high.

Place each fillet horizontally in front of you. Starting at the left end, put your knife at a 45-degree angle to cut against the grain (in other words, the lines of sinew running through the fillet—if you cut in the same direction as them, the fish will fall apart). Tilt the top edge of the knife to the right in order to cut at a sharp angle down toward the left. Cut the entire fillet into thin slices, about ⅓ in [8 mm] thick (some people like it thinner).

Serve immediately with wasabi, soy sauce in a bowl, and, if you like, some sticky Japanese rice.

PERFECT RIB OF BEEF

Wonderful meat, simply roasted. Serve with friends.

INGREDIENTS (SERVES 8)

1 x well-aged 3- or 4-rib of beef
(about 11 lb [5 kg] on the bone)
Groundnut oil, for rubbing
1½ cups [350 ml] red wine

ROAST POTATOES:

3 lb [1.5 kg] medium-large mealy potatoes
1¼ cups [300 ml] groundnut oil
½ cup [50 g] flour, for dusting
1 head of garlic (optional)
3 fresh rosemary sprigs (optional)
Salt and black pepper

METHOD—Preheat the oven to 475°F [240°C]. Rub the meat all over with a little oil and season with salt and pepper. Put it in a large roasting tin and roast in the oven 25 minutes, then reduce the heat to 325°F [170°C]. For a 11 lb [5 kg] rib of beef, cook 3 hours for medium rare. Add up to 50 minutes longer to get it well-done—if you really must. The rules of thumb for cooking times are: 30 minutes plus 30 minutes per 2¼ lb [1 kg] for medium rare, or 30 minutes plus 40 minutes per 2¼ lb [1 kg] for well done.

Meanwhile, make the roast potatoes. Heat a pan of water large enough to hold all the potatoes easily. Add ½ tsp salt. Cut the potatoes into 1½ to 2 in [4 to 5 cm] chunks. There is nothing precise about this and the exact size is up to you. Remember, though, that the potatoes will shrink a little during cooking, and that chunks with thinnish, sharp edges will caramelize more than square-cut chunks. Put them in the boiling water and simmer gently about 6 minutes—they should be firm at the center.

Heat the oven to its highest setting and pour the oil in a large roasting tin—it should be big enough for the potatoes not to be overcrowded. Put the tin in the oven. Drain the potatoes carefully in a colander, shaking them gently to fluff up the exteriors. Sift the flour, seasoned generously with salt and pepper, over the top and shake again. Pile the potatoes carefully into your roasting tin of hot oil and spoon a little oil over each one so they are all well coated and return to the hot oven. After 5 minutes, reduce the temperature to 425°F [220°C] and roast 50 minutes, or until your potatoes are beautifully golden with patches of orangey brown. Turn them once or twice during cooking. If using garlic, separate out the cloves, keeping them in their skins, and add them after 25 minutes. If using rosemary, strip the leaves and add to the tin after 45 minutes.

Remove the beef from the oven and cover with aluminum foil. Leave to rest at least 20 minutes before carving. To make the sauce, deglaze the roasting tin with the red wine, scraping the bottom of the pan to dissolve the sediment, and simmer gently over medium heat to reduce a little. Serve with roast potatoes, vegetables, mustard, and horseradish.

MOUSSAKA

INGREDIENTS (SERVES 4)

LAMB SHOULDER:

1 x 2¼ lb [1 kg] lamb shoulder

1 cup [250 ml] white wine

MOUSSAKA:

3 large eggplants, cut into ⅜ in [1 cm] thick slices

14 Tbsp [200 ml] olive oil

1 large onion, finely chopped

3 garlic cloves, crushed

⅝ cup [150 ml] dry white wine

1 cinnamon stick

¼ tsp ground allspice

2 tsp fresh or dried wild marjoram or oregano

1⅛ lb [500 g] tomatoes, skinned and chopped

Salt and black pepper

TOPPING:

1 onion

2½ cups [600 ml] milk

1 bay leaf

2 cloves

5 black peppercorns

4½ Tbsp [70 g] butter

7 Tbsp [70 g] flour

1¼ cup [100 g] kefalotyri cheese, grated (or use
  Parmesan or pecorino)

¼ tsp grated nutmeg

2 eggs, beaten

Salt and white pepper

METHOD—Start by preparing the meat. Preheat the oven to 325°F [170°C]. Put the lamb shoulder in a roasting tin and pour over the wine. Season with salt and pepper. Braise in the oven, covered with foil, about 2 hours, or until very tender, basting occasionally. Remove from the oven and remove most of the fat, then shred the meat finely and set it aside.

Salt the eggplant slices and put them in a colander on a plate or over the sink to let the bitter juices drain away.

Heat 2 Tbsp oil in a large pan, add the onion, and cook for a few minutes until softened. Add the garlic. Increase the heat and add the lamb meat, season with salt and pepper, and fry it on all sides until slightly browned, and any liquid in the pan has evaporated. Now add the wine, cinnamon stick, allspice, herbs, and tomatoes. Reduce the heat and simmer 30 to 40 minutes (it should not be too liquid by the end), before removing the cinnamon stick.

Heat the milk in a pan and add the whole onion, bay leaf, cloves, and a few black peppercorns. Bring the milk to a boil, remove, and set aside to infuse.

Rinse the eggplants and pat them dry thoroughly with paper towels. Heat the remaining oil in a large skillet until it is sizzling hot and add the eggplant slices in batches. Fry until golden on both sides. Drain on a plate lined with paper towels.

Preheat the oven to 400°F [200°C]. Remove the onion and spices from the milk and reheat it. In another pan, melt the butter over medium heat and add the flour. Cook for a minute, whisking vigorously, then add the hot milk, one ladle at a time, continuing to whisk. Once all the milk has been added, bring to a boil and cook for a few minutes, until thick. Add the grated cheese and nutmeg and stir well. Season with salt and white pepper and remove from the heat. Once the cheese has melted and the sauce has cooled slightly, whisk in the beaten eggs.

In a 8 x 12 in [20 x 30 cm] ovenproof dish, arrange half of the eggplants over the base. Spread half the meat sauce on top. Add another layer of eggplants and meat sauce, and finish by pouring over the cheese topping. Bake 30 to 40 minutes, or until golden. Cover with aluminum foil if it colors too quickly. Let stand for a little before serving.

BEEF IN BAROLO

INGREDIENTS (SERVES 6)

2¼ lb [1 kg] beef fillet
1 onion, chopped
1 celery stalk, chopped
1 carrot, chopped
1 bay leaf
1 fresh rosemary sprig
10 black peppercorns
3¼ cups [750 ml] Barolo
2 Tbsp butter
2 Tbsp oil
2 Tbsp raw fatty ham or prosciutto, chopped
1 small square bitter chocolate (optional)
1 tsp cornstarch
Salt and black pepper

This is an über-elegant dinner-party dish. Above all, don't scrimp on the quality of the wine: spend your money here. A mature and elegant Barolo is a truly great wine that suffuses this dish with an amazing depth of flavor.

METHOD—Put the meat in a bowl and add the onion, celery, carrot, herbs, and peppercorns. Pour in the wine and marinate 24 hours in the refrigerator.

Remove the beef, reserving the marinade, pat it dry and tie it with kitchen string so it keeps its shape during cooking.

Heat the butter and oil in a casserole dish, add the chopped ham, and cook until golden. Add the beef and brown it well on all sides. Add the marinade and vegetables and season with salt. A piece of bitter chocolate can be added, if you like, to soften the wine's acidity. Cover and simmer over low heat until the meat is tender—about 1½ hours.

When the meat is tender, remove it and set aside. Remove the herbs and press the sauce and vegetables through a fine sieve. If the sauce is too liquid, dissolve the cornstarch in a little water, add it to the sauce, and bring to a boil to thicken. Remove the string from the beef and slice it thinly. Arrange on a platter and spoon the sauce over it to serve.

WHOLE ROAST TURBOT

INGREDIENTS (SERVES 4)

2¼ lb [1 kg] potatoes

5 Tbsp olive oil, plus extra for drizzling

1 x 4½ lb [2 kg] turbot, gutted

1 fresh thyme sprig

2 garlic cloves, finely chopped

1 Tbsp fresh flat-leaf parsley, leaves chopped

Grated zest of ½ lemon

3 tomatoes, thinly sliced

2 tsp capers

¼ cup [60 ml] dry white wine

Salt and black pepper

METHOD—Preheat the oven to 350°F [180°C]. Using a Chinese mandolin or a very sharp kitchen knife, slice the potatoes very thinly. Place them in a bowl, season with salt and pepper, and mix with the olive oil. Coat well and transfer three-quarters of them to a large baking pan or a shallow oven tray, spreading them out evenly to the edges.

Wash the turbot and pat it dry. Season with salt and pepper on both sides. Put the thyme in the cavity and place it on the bed of potatoes. Combine the garlic, parsley, and lemon zest with a little oil and spread it over the fish. Add the tomato slices and the capers. Pour the wine around the fish. Cover the turbot with the remaining potato slices and drizzle a little olive oil over the top. Bake in the oven 45 minutes, or until lightly golden.

When ready to serve, gently pull the skin off the turbot. Lift off the fillets with a knife and remove the central bone to access the low-lying fillets. Serve with the potatoes and the juices from the pan.

ONE-POT CHICKEN

INGREDIENTS (SERVES 6)

1 x 2¼ lb [1 kg] chicken

3 carrots, cut into large chunks

2 onions, halved

1 leek, cut into large chunks

1 celery heart, cut into large chunks

2 small turnips, cut into large chunks

¼ Savoy cabbage, cut into large chunks

6 garlic cloves

3 fresh thyme sprigs

2 cups [500 ml] white wine

2 cups [500 ml] light chicken stock

Salt and black pepper

METHOD—Preheat the oven to 425°F [220°C]. You'll need a casserole dish large enough to hold all the ingredients snugly. Put the chicken in the casserole breast-side down and add the vegetables, thyme, wine, stock, and about 2 cups [500 ml] water—you want the liquid to come two-thirds of the way up the chicken. Season with salt and pepper. Bring to a boil over high heat. Cover and transfer to the oven.

After 30 minutes, carefully turn the chicken over, put the lid back on and cook a further 40 minutes. Remove the lid for the last 10 minutes of cooking to brown the top of the chicken lightly.

Carve the chicken into pieces and serve with some vegetables on each plate, ladling the broth over the top. Accompany with plain rice, boiled potatoes, or good bread.

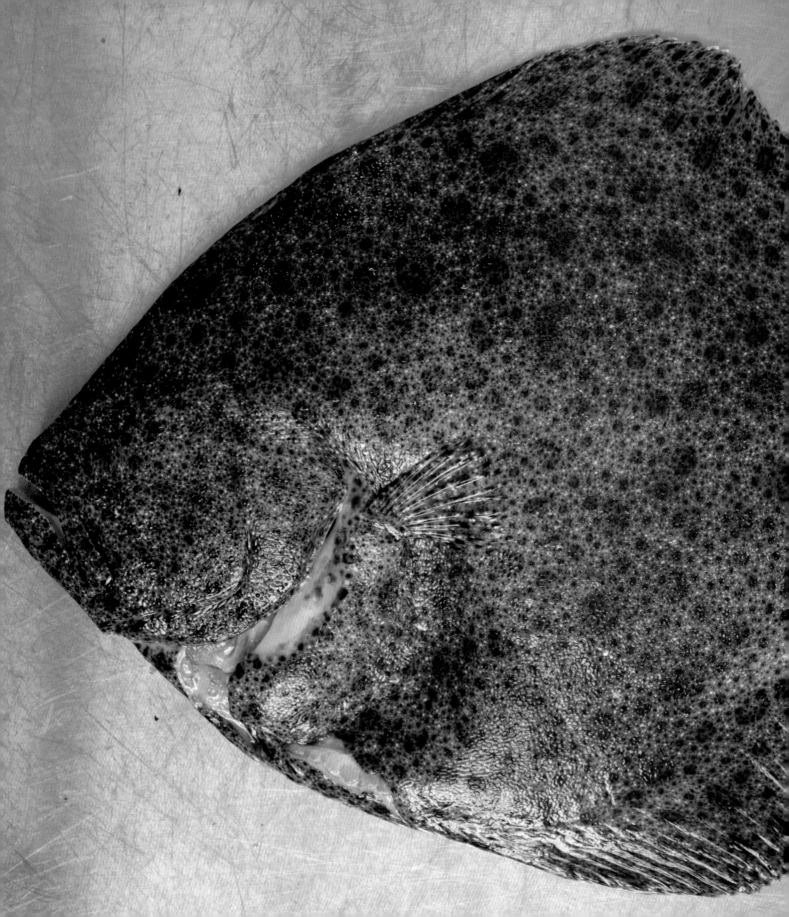

OSSO BUCO

Italy wins gold again!

INGREDIENTS (SERVES 4)

4 pieces veal shank cut from the hind leg,
about 1½ in [4 cm] thick

1 Tbsp flour

3 Tbsp vegetable oil

4 Tbsp butter

1 onion, finely chopped

½ garlic clove, finely chopped

1 carrot, finely chopped

1 celery stalk, finely chopped

14 Tbsp [200 ml] dry white wine

7 oz [200 g] canned tomatoes

1 bay leaf

1 strip lemon zest (optional)

Salt and black pepper

GREMOLATA:

1 bunch fresh flat-leaf parsley, finely chopped

1 garlic clove, finely chopped

Finely grated zest of 1 lemon

METHOD—Thoroughly dust the meat with the flour on all sides. Heat a little oil in a casserole dish over medium heat, add the meat, and brown it. Remove it and set aside. Melt the butter in the pan, add the onion, garlic, carrot, and celery and cook until lightly golden. Place the meat on top of the vegetables, add the wine, and let it evaporate. Press the tomatoes through a sieve and add them to the pan. Add the bay leaf and season with salt and pepper. If you're not planning to make the gremolata, add the lemon zest too. The liquid should come two-thirds of the way up the sides of the meat— add some hot water if necessary. Cover, bring to a boil, skim the sauce, and simmer over medium heat about 1½ hours. Turn the meat occasionally; it should become very tender and detach from the bone.

For the gremolata, mix the parsley and garlic with the lemon zest. Spread the mixture sparingly over the shanks and do not turn them again. Leave to infuse about 3 minutes, then remove from the heat.

Transfer the shanks to a warm platter and pour the sauce over it (if it is too liquid, reduce the sauce a little over a high heat). Serve piping hot with risotto or plain rice.

FISH SOUP
WITH ROUILLE

INGREDIENTS (SERVES 8)
SOUP:

7 Tbsp [100 ml] olive oil

1 onion, chopped

5 garlic cloves, crushed

1 fennel bulb, chopped

1 leek, sliced

2¼ lb [1 kg] mixed fish, such as gurnard, monkfish, John Dory, red mullet, gutted, trimmed, and cut into pieces (keep the heads)

2¼ lb [1 kg] mixed swimming crab and small shrimp

3½ oz [100 g] tomato paste

10½ oz [300 g] tomatoes, chopped

½ tsp saffron threads

Zest of 1 orange

1 bouquet garni (consisting of 2 bay leaves, 4 fresh thyme sprigs, 6 fresh flat-leaf parsley sprigs, 1 star anise, 6 white peppercorns)

½ cup [120 ml] white wine

3 Tbsp Pernod

Salt and black pepper

ROUILLE:

1 small onion

2 egg yolks

1 cup [250 ml] olive oil

2 garlic cloves, crushed with ½ tsp salt

1 tsp cayenne pepper

2 baguettes, sliced, to serve

Fish soup is common fare in southern France, and there are as many regional varieties as there are villages around the coast. Don't worry too much about which type of fish to use—remember that the fishermen just used whatever they had left over from their day's catch.

METHOD—Heat the oil in a large casserole dish and cook the onions, garlic, fennel, and leek 5 minutes, until soft, stirring occasionally. Add the fish heads, any trimmings, fish pieces, crabs, and shrimp and simmer 5 minutes before adding the tomato paste, tomatoes, saffron, orange zest, bouquet garni, wine, and Pernod. Season with salt and pepper and cover with about 4½ qt [4 L] cold water. Simmer over low heat 40 minutes.

Meanwhile, prepare the rouille. Start by peeling the onion and pushing it firmly onto a fork. This will be your utensil. Place the egg yolks in a small, nonmetallic bowl and begin to stir with the onioned fork. Little by little, add the olive oil, stirring continuously. Once the oil and yolk have amalgamated well into a nice, creamy texture, add the garlic, salt, and cayenne pepper, and stir. Toast the baguette slices.

When the soup is cooked, remove the bouquet garni and pass the soup through a mouli or food mill. If you don't have one, strain the liquid into a bowl and crush the fish heads, bones, and shells as much as possible, then add all the fish to the strainer and press out as much juice as you can with a large spoon. Return the soup to the pan and keep it hot while preparing the toasts and rouille. Serve hot with toasted baguette slices and the rouille.

PAELLA
WITH RABBIT & BEANS

The correct preparation of Valencian-style paella is a subject of much heated debate. Some versions call for additional chicken meat, others snails. It's said that the usage of bell peppers was even discussed before the city's parliament. Well, purism is a bore, and I've added bell peppers and artichokes to my version.

INGREDIENTS (SERVES 4)

Olive oil, for frying
1 rabbit, jointed
2 large onions, diced
5 garlic cloves, crushed
1 yellow bell pepper, seeded and cut into thin strips
8¾ oz [250 g] Calasparra rice
½ tsp sweet smoked paprika
⅝ cup [150 ml] dry sherry or white wine
3⅓ cups [800 ml] chicken stock
½ tsp saffron threads
7 oz [200 g] shelled fresh fava beans
3 small grilled artichoke hearts in oil,
  drained and quartered (optional)
Lemon juice, to taste
1 Tbsp fresh flat-leaf parsley, leaves chopped
Salt and black pepper

METHOD—Heat the olive oil in a large paella pan. Fry the rabbit until nicely browned on all sides, then remove and set aside. Add the onions and soften 15 minutes over medium heat, then add the garlic and pepper. Cook another 10 minutes, until soft. Add the rice and paprika and heat through for 1 minute. Increase the heat. Add the sherry or wine and let evaporate. Now add the stock and saffron; season with salt and pepper and simmer 10 minutes, without stirring.

Add the rabbit and simmer 10 minutes more. Meanwhile, soak the shelled beans in boiling water for 2 minutes, before draining them. Squeeze to remove the outer skin of the beans.

When the paella is ready, scatter the beans and artichokes on top and cover with aluminum foil. Leave to stand 10 minutes, remove the foil, add the lemon juice and chopped parsley, and serve.

CRAB
WITH CHILI
& BLACK BEAN SAUCE

This dish is eaten with your hands. It's messy.

INGREDIENTS (SERVES 4)

2 large live brown crabs

1 Tbsp groundnut oil

2 garlic cloves, crushed

1 Tbsp fresh ginger root, grated

1 large, mild red chili, finely sliced

1 Tbsp soy sauce

1½ tsp brown sugar

2 Tbsp rice wine vinegar

¾ cup [170 ml] chicken stock

3 Tbsp dried black beans

4 scallions, sliced into shards

METHOD—Butcher and prepare your crabs. Put them in the freezer for 20 minutes, so they become drowsy. To kill a crab, place it on its back. Lift the triangular-shaped tail flap. There's a small indentation. Drive a sharp knife or chopstick with one forceful blow through to the chopping board. Next, do the same just below the eyes. Pull off the tail flap. Turn over and press from underneath onto the middle and the leg area. Pull off the top shell. Cut off the dead man's fingers (gills) and remove the stomach sac from behind the mouth. Cut the crab into quarters. Finally, crack the claws by hitting them with a mallet.

Place a wok or skillet (with lid) over medium heat and add the oil. Now add the garlic, ginger, and chili and fry for up to 1 minute. Be careful not to burn the garlic. Add the soy sauce, brown sugar, rice wine vinegar, stock, and dried black beans. Bring to a boil and add the crab pieces. Cover, reduce the heat, and simmer 15 minutes. Serve the crab heaped in a large bowl with the sauce poured over and the scallions scattered on top. Serve with a bowl of warm water with lemon slices in it for hand cleaning afterward.

ZAKUSKI

Zakuski are the little snacks that Russians serve with vodka that's been chilled to within an inch of its life. The spread can be as lavish or as simple as you like. It's good to have a mix of hot and cold dishes, and also a combination of fish, vegetables, and meat. Bread should be served, rye bread traditionally. There must also be pickles and cold cuts of some sort. The dishes given here could be supplemented with a little caviar or lumpfish roe, cured herring (see p. 211) with raw onions, smoked salmon, or perhaps gravadlax (not Russian, but good, see p. 201), or a meat borscht (see p. 79). For your own good, follow these two rules: 1. You must not mix your drinks. 2. Vodka should be sipped rather than chugged. *Nostrovia!*

RUSSIAN EGGS
INGREDIENTS

6 hard-boiled eggs, halved lengthwise

2 Tbsp crème fraîche

1 heaped tsp Dijon mustard

2 tsp chopped fresh chives

1 tsp lemon juice

Pinch of cayenne pepper

6 tsp salmon roe or caviar (optional)

Salt

METHOD—Carefully remove the yolks from the eggs and place in a bowl. Finely mash them with a fork and add the crème fraîche, mustard, chives, and lemon juice. Season with salt and cayenne pepper. Fill the egg white halves with the yolk mixture, using a spoon or piping bag. If you like, top each half with some fish roe.

BEET & WALNUT SALAD
INGREDIENTS

4 beets

6 prunes

Cooled black tea, for soaking

¾ cup [80 g] walnuts, chopped

2 garlic cloves, finely chopped

1 tsp lemon juice

3 Tbsp Greek yogurt

Salt and black pepper

METHOD—Put the whole, unpeeled beets in a pan and cover with plenty of water. Cover and bring to a boil. Simmer 1 to 2 hours, depending on the size, until tender. Insert a sharp knife to test this. Drain, let cool for a few minutes, then rub the skin off with paper towels.

Soak the prunes 1 hour in a weak black tea infusion, then chop them. Grate the beets and mix them together with the prunes, walnuts, and garlic. Add the lemon juice and yogurt. Stir and season with salt and pepper. Cover with plastic wrap and leave to infuse in the refrigerator at least 2 hours.

ZAKUSKI CONTINUED

MUSHROOM CAVIAR
INGREDIENTS

- 1⅛ lb [500 g] mushrooms (such as fresh ceps or Portobello), trimmed
- 2 Tbsp butter
- 2 Tbsp vegetable oil
- Juice of ½ lemon
- 2 shallots, finely chopped
- 2 garlic cloves, finely chopped
- ⅝ cup [150 ml] smetana (Russian sour cream) or crème fraîche
- 2 Tbsp chopped fresh dill
- Salt and black pepper

METHOD—Remove the stalks from the mushrooms. Quarter the heads and chop the stalks. Heat half the butter and oil in a skillet over high heat. When the pan is very hot, add the quartered mushroom heads and toss them quickly all over in the fat. Cook 2 minutes, reduce the heat (if a lot of liquid comes out, wait until it has evaporated) and fry another 3 minutes, or until nicely browned. Squeeze the lemon juice over. Remove the mushrooms and set aside.

Add the shallots, garlic, and chopped stalks to the pan with the remaining butter and oil. Cook 10 minutes, then return the mushroom heads, add the sour cream, and dill. Season with salt and pepper. Serve at room temperature.

BLINIS
INGREDIENTS (MAKES 12)

- ⅝ cup [70 g] buckwheat flour, sifted
- ⅝ cup [70 g] all-purpose flour, sifted
- ½ tsp salt
- 1 tsp dried yeast
- ½ tsp sugar
- ¾ cup [175 ml] milk, lukewarm
- 1 large egg, separated
- 1 Tbsp butter, melted
- Vegetable oil, for frying

METHOD—In a large mixing bowl, combine the 2 flours with the salt. Make a well in the middle. Dissolve the yeast and sugar in half the lukewarm milk. Leave for 5 minutes until the yeast bubbles up. Pour it into the well in the flour and whisk together. Leave to rest 30 minutes.

Gently heat the remaining milk, add the egg yolk, and whisk. Add to the yeast-flour mixture with 1 Tbsp melted butter. Stir well and leave to rest 45 minutes.

Beat the egg white until it forms soft peaks, then gently fold it into the batter. Leave to rest 30 minutes more.

Lightly grease a nonstick skillet with a little oil and place over medium heat. When the pan is hot, ladle 1 Tbsp batter into the pan and fry about 1 minute, until little bubbles burst on the surface. Turn over and fry another 30 seconds.

Keep them warm wrapped in a clean dish towel while you fry the rest of the blinis. If you plan to serve them later, reheat them for 15 minutes in the oven at 325°F [170°C]. Serve with sour cream and your chosen topping.

JAMBALAYA

INGREDIENTS (SERVES 6)

1 chicken, jointed into 8 pieces

Vegetable oil, for frying

8¾ oz [250 g] andouille sausage, or other smoked pork
  sausage (such as chorizo), sliced

1 onion, chopped

2 celery stalks, chopped

1 green bell pepper, seeded and chopped

1 hot red chili, chopped

2 garlic cloves, chopped

7 oz [200 g] tomatoes, skinned and chopped

4 bay leaves

4½ cups [1 L] chicken stock

14 oz [400 g] long-grain rice, rinsed and drained

18 large raw shrimp or crayfish tails, peeled

Squeeze of lemon juice

4 tsp fresh flat-leaf parsley, leaves chopped

Salt

CREOLE HOT SPICE MIX:

3½ oz [100 g] salt

3 Tbsp black pepper

2 Tbsp white pepper

2 Tbsp Cayenne pepper

2 Tbsp garlic powder

2 Tbsp onion powder

2 Tbsp parsley flakes

2 Tbsp paprika

1 Tbsp dried thyme

Jambalaya means "jumbled-up," and you should approach this dish in that spirit.

METHOD—First, prepare the spice mix: combine all the ingredients in a food processor and grind to a powder, then set aside.

Place the chicken pieces in a large mixing bowl and add 3 Tbsp Creole hot spice powder. Toss well.

Heat a few Tbsp oil in a large casserole dish or shallow skillet. Add the chicken pieces and brown on all sides over a high heat for about 10 minutes. Remove and set aside. Now fry the sausage slices for 5 minutes, then remove and set aside.

Add a little more oil if necessary, then add the onion, celery, and pepper. Cook over medium heat 10 minutes, until soft, then add the red chili and garlic. After 2 minutes, return the chicken and sausage to the pan, then add the tomatoes, bay leaves, and chicken stock. Cover and simmer 20 minutes.

Add the rice and cook another 15 minutes, giving it an occasional stir. Once the rice is cooked, add the shrimp, stir well, cover, and cook for a final 10 minutes. Squeeze some lemon juice over the top and sprinkle with the chopped parsley to serve.

PEKING DUCK

In my experience, "sharing" this dish is an intensely competitive activity.

INGREDIENTS (SERVES 4)

1 x 5½ lb [2.5 kg] duck

7 oz [200 g] maltose (or 3 Tbsp honey)

1 Tbsp white wine vinegar

5 Tbsp rice wine

3 Tbsp dark soy sauce

20 Mandarin pancakes

4 scallions, cut into thin matchsticks

½ cucumber, cut into thin matchsticks

PLUM SAUCE:

10 plums

3 garlic cloves, chopped

½ Tbsp fresh ginger root, chopped

¼ tsp hot chili powder

2 Tbsp dark soy sauce

5 tsp sugar

METHOD—Clean the duck and remove any excess fat from the cavity. Pat it dry inside and outside. Very carefully loosen the duck's skin by pushing your hand between the flesh and skin all the way round it.

Bring 4½ cups [1 L] water to the boil and stir in the maltose or honey. Add the vinegar, rice wine, and soy sauce. Attach the duck's neck to a butcher's hook, or make a hook with a coat hanger. Holding the duck in the air over the pan to catch any drips, ladle the glaze over the duck repeatedly for about 10 minutes. When the duck is completely glazed, find a cool and airy place to hang it (ideally with a fan blowing). Let dry for at least 6 hours, or even better, overnight.

Preheat the oven to 475°F [240°C]. Place the duck on a roasting rack, with a roasting tin containing 2 cups [500 ml] boiling water underneath it, and cook in the oven 10 minutes. Reduce the temperature to 350°F [180°C] and cook another 70 minutes.

Meanwhile, make the plum sauce. Stone and chop the plums. Put them in a saucepan together with the rest of the ingredients and add a little water. Bring to a boil, cover, and simmer 10 to 15 minutes, stirring occasionally. Process in a blender and let cool. Add a little more water if the consistency is too thick.

Remove the duck from the oven and let cool for a few minutes to allow the glaze to harden. Using a sharp knife, shave off the skin and shred the meat. Place on a platter and serve with Mandarin pancakes (heated gently in a skillet, or steamed), plum sauce, scallions, and cucumber.

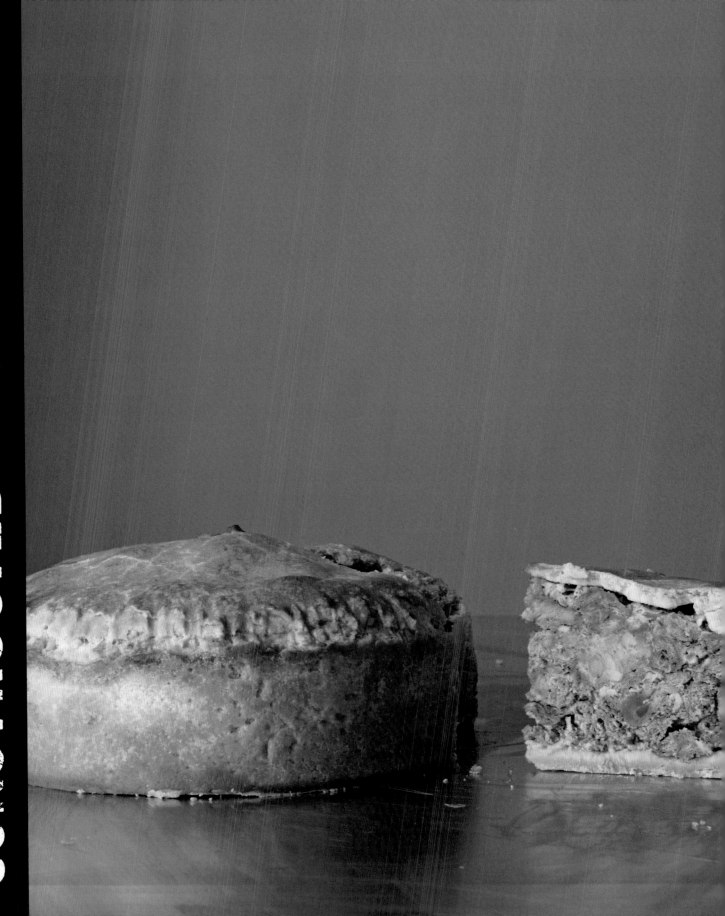

PORK PIE

INGREDIENTS (SERVES 6)

FILLING:

2¼ lb [1 kg] boned pork shoulder (bones reserved),
   cut into ¼ in [5 mm] cubes

8¾ oz [250 g] unsmoked bacon, rindless

5 fresh sage leaves, finely chopped

2 canned anchovy fillets, finely chopped

¼ tsp ground nutmeg

½ tsp ground allspice

2 tsp salt

1 tsp ground black pepper

PASTRY:

¾ cup [180 g] lard or butter, plus extra for greasing

4 cups [500 g] flour

1 tsp salt

1 egg, beaten

STOCK:

2 pig's trotters or 1 veal knuckle

2 carrots, sliced

1 onion stuck with 2 cloves

10 black peppercorns

1 bouquet garni

METHOD—Prepare the stock. Put the pork bones, pig's trotters, or veal knuckle in a large casserole dish with the vegetables, peppercorns, and bouquet garni. Add cold water to cover and bring to a boil over medium heat. Reduce the heat, skim to remove any impurities, and simmer gently 2 hours. Strain through a fine sieve. Bring the stock back to a boil in a clean pan and reduce it until you have about 1½ cups [350 ml] liquid left; let cool. Do not let it set solid; if that happens, warm it through slightly.

For the filling, process half the pork in a blender until smooth. Combine the meats in a bowl with the bacon, sage, anchovies, spices, and salt and pepper. Add 3 Tbsp of the stock and stir well. Cover with plastic wrap and leave to chill in the refrigerator while you prepare the pastry.

Preheat the oven to 350°F [180°C]. Lightly grease an 8 in [20 cm] nonstick cake tin or pie mold.

Make the pastry. Sieve the flour into a mixing bowl and add the salt. Place the lard and 14 Tbsp [200 ml] water in a pan and bring to a boil. Add the liquid to the flour and stir vigorously with a wooden spoon. Once the mixture is amalgamated, transfer it to a work surface and knead it quickly until smooth. The dough must remain warm when you roll it out, so you need to work quite fast.

Roll out about two-thirds of the dough and use it to line the prepared tin or molds, starting at the base and gently pressing it up the sides. Make sure the dough does not tear and that there are no gaps or holes, and leave an overhang of a fraction of an inch. Roll out the remaining third of the dough to make a neatly fitting lid. Fill the tin with the pork mixture—it should come almost all the way up to the rim. Brush the rim and the overhang with the beaten egg and place the lid on top, pressing around the edges firmly with a fork, or crimping with your thumb and index finger. Cut a small hole in the center of the lid. Brush the top with the remaining egg and bake in the oven about 1 hour.

To check whether the pie is ready, insert a skewer into the hole in the middle of the pie, leave for a few seconds, then remove and check if it is hot all the way along. The crust should also have a good golden color. Remove from the tin and let cool on a rack.

Pour the reserved, reduced stock through the hole in the lid, using a funnel, and let cool completely before chilling the pie in the refrigerator for a day before serving.

BEEF, ALE & OYSTER PIE

The addition of oysters to this pie dates back to a time when they where cheaper than meat and used as a filler. The pie is delicious with or without them.

INGREDIENTS (SERVES 6)
FILLING:

3 Tbsp vegetable oil

2¼ lb [1 kg] braising steak, cut into chunks

3 onions, diced

3 carrots, thickly sliced

3 Tbsp flour

3 fresh thyme sprigs

2 bay leaves

2 cups [500 ml] dark ale

1 cup [250 ml] beef stock

10½ oz [300 g] button mushrooms, quartered

12 oysters (optional)

Salt and black pepper

ROUGH PUFF PASTRY:

1 tsp salt

3¼ cups [400 g] flour, sieved, plus extra for dusting

1¾ cups [400 g] cold butter, diced, plus extra for greasing

1 egg yolk, beaten

METHOD—First, make the pastry. Mix the salt into the flour and place on a clean work surface. Add the diced butter and coat with the flour, breaking the butter into smaller pieces with your fingers. Gradually add 14 Tbsp [200 ml] cold water. Lightly knead until you have a rough dough with visible lumps of butter in it—do not overwork it. Wrap in plastic wrap and let rest 15 minutes in the refrigerator.

Dust the work surface with flour and roll out the pastry into a long rectangle, rolling only in one direction. Fold one third into the middle and fold the other end over it to form a sandwich. Turn it through 90 degrees, roll it out into a long rectangle once more, and fold into three in the same way. Chill 30 minutes, then repeat the rolling and folding procedure twice more. Chill at least 30 minutes.

Preheat the oven to 300°F [150°C]. Heat the oil in a large casserole dish, add the beef in batches (if you overcrowd the pan, the meat may boil rather than fry), and brown on all sides. Remove and set aside. Add the onions and cook about 5 minutes, until softened. Add the carrots and cook a further 3 minutes.

Return the beef to the casserole. Season with salt and pepper and sprinkle with the flour. Stir well, and after another minute add the herbs, ale, and stock. Cover and cook in the oven 2 hours. Add the button mushrooms for the last 15 minutes of cooking.

If using, shuck the oysters and set aside. Preheat the oven to 375°F [190°C]. Grease a 10 in [26 cm] pie mold.

Remove the pastry from the refrigerator and roll out two-thirds of it to a similar shape to your pie dish, but slightly bigger. Line the dish with the pastry. Press it firmly onto the edges and cut off any overhang. Using a slotted spoon, fill the pie with the beef stew. Don't add too much of the liquid. Next, add the oysters, if using, and push them down into the filling. The pie should be completely filled. Roll out the remaining dough to make a lid. Brush the edges of the pastry with the egg and place the lid over the top. Trim off any overhang and crimp around the rim firmly with your thumb and fingers. Make a few incisions in the lid with a sharp knife and brush with the egg. Bake in the oven 50 minutes, or until golden. Serve hot.

LAMB SAMOSAS

INGREDIENTS (MAKES APPROXIMATELY 24)
DOUGH:

2 cups [250 g] flour, plus extra for dusting

1 tsp salt

¼ tsp ajwain seeds (optional)

3 Tbsp groundnut oil

FILLING:

3 Tbsp vegetable oil

1 onion, chopped

2 garlic cloves, crushed

2 green chilies, finely chopped

¾ in [2 cm] fresh ginger root, grated

1 tsp ground cumin

½ tsp ground coriander

½ tsp turmeric

1 tsp garam masala

1⅛ lb [500 g] ground lamb

Large handful fresh cilantro leaves, chopped

Vegetable oil, for frying

METHOD—To make the dough, combine the flour, salt, and ajwain seeds, if using, in a bowl. Add the oil little by little, rubbing it in with your fingers. You need to achieve a grainy texture. Gradually add a little lukewarm water (you'll need around ⅓ cup [80 ml] in total) and combine to make a dough—don't use too much, as the pastry easily becomes too sticky. Knead until smooth and pliable. Leave to rest for 15 minutes.

For the filling, heat a little oil in a skillet over low heat. Add the onion and cook 5 minutes, until soft, before adding the garlic. Cook for another minute, then add the chilies and spices. After 2 minutes, add the lamb and increase the heat. Fry, stirring, until browned. When the released liquid has almost evaporated, add 7 Tbsp [100 ml] boiling water, cover and simmer 15 minutes. Remove the lid, increase the heat, and continue to simmer about 5 minutes, until the meat is tender and moist, but no liquid is left in the pan. Stir in the cilantro leaves.

Divide the dough into 12 small pieces. Lightly dust a work surface with flour and roll out into oval shapes. Cut in half widthwise. Moisten the edges with water and bring one corner to the center. Fold over the other corner to make a cone shape. Spoon in some of the filling and fold over the rounded edge. Crimp firmly.

Heat the vegetable oil in a deep pan or deep-fat fryer to 300°F [150°C]. Fry the samosas in batches until golden brown. Remove and drain on paper towels before serving with chutney.

PORK, CHICKEN & HERB TERRINE

INGREDIENTS (SERVES 8)

2 lb [900 g] boned pork shoulder

⅝ cup [150 ml] heavy cream

1 tsp fresh thyme leaves, chopped

3 Tbsp brandy

3 Tbsp Marsala

1 egg, beaten

2 chicken breasts

8¾ oz [250 g] bacon rashers

2 Tbsp chopped fresh chives

2 Tbsp chopped fresh tarragon

3 Tbsp chopped fresh flat-leaf parsley

Salt and black pepper

METHOD—If you have a meat grinder, grind the pork through the medium blade twice. If not, ask your butcher to grind it for you, medium-fine.

Put the pork in a bowl and stir in the cream, thyme, brandy, Marsala, and egg, and season with salt and pepper. Fry a small piece of the mixture and taste it to check the seasoning, then set aside in the refrigerator.

Slice the chicken breasts into strips. Arrange a large sheet of plastic wrap on a clean work surface and place 2 rashers of bacon on it without touching. Put another sheet of plastic wrap on top and gently use a rolling pin to roll out the bacon until thin but not falling apart. Repeat with the rest of the bacon.

Line a 3 lb [1.5 kg] terrine or loaf tin with the bacon so that the bottom and sides are covered and there is enough bacon hanging over the edges to be able to fold over and cover the contents. Mix together the rest of the herbs. Seasoning with salt and pepper between each layer, put half the pork mixture in the terrine, spreading it out evenly, sprinkle over a layer of herbs, then make a layer of all the chicken, then finally the rest of the pork mixture. Fold over the bacon to cover. Chill 2 hours.

Preheat the oven to 350°F [180°C]. Cover the terrine with aluminum foil. Place it in a large roasting tin and half-fill the tin with boiling water. Cook in the oven 40 to 45 minutes. Remove and place a board on top, and weight it with about 9 oz [250 g] to compress gently until it has completely cooled. There should be a good amount of liquid, which will set when it chills, and it will have shrunk a little. Chill in the refrigerator before serving.

COARSE COUNTRY PÂTÉ

This is a classic taste of France and extremely easy to make.

INGREDIENTS (SERVES 10)

1¾ lb [800 g] pork shoulder, bones, cartilage, and skin removed, coarsely chopped

14 oz [400 g] bacon, chopped

2 shallots, chopped

7 Tbsp [100 ml] dry white wine

3 Tbsp Cognac

3 Tbsp Madeira

1 bay leaf

2 cloves

1 fresh rosemary sprig

1 fresh thyme sprig

2 eggs, beaten

¼ tsp ground allspice

Pinch of nutmeg

1 garlic clove, crushed

1 tsp fresh thyme leaves

Caul fat, soaked in cold water (alternatively, use 12 bacon rashers)

Butter, for greasing

Salt and black pepper

METHOD—Place the meat and bacon in a mixing bowl. Add the shallots, wine, Cognac, Madeira, bay leaf, cloves, rosemary, and thyme. Cover with plastic wrap and leave to marinate in the refrigerator overnight.

Remove the bay leaf, rosemary, cloves, and thyme and discard. Run the meat with the liquid through a meat grinder, using the medium blade, and place it in a mixing bowl. Add the eggs, allspice, nutmeg, garlic, and thyme and season with salt and pepper. Stir well.

Preheat the oven to 300°F [150°C]. Rinse the caul fat, if using. Grease a 2 lb [900 g] loaf tin or terrine mold and line it with the caul fat or bacon rashers, leaving a little overhang along the rim. Fill the terrine with the pork mixture and fold over the caul fat or rashers to cover the filling. Cover with aluminum foil.

Place the terrine in a larger roasting tin filled with hot water (it should come halfway up the sides of the terrine). Cook in the oven 3 hours. Remove the foil for the last 30 minutes of cooking. Take the terrine out of the oven, let cool, and chill in the refrigerator for 2 days before serving. Serve with bread and pickles.

CHICKEN LIVER PÂTÉ

This melting pâté is quick to prepare and delicious.

INGREDIENTS (SERVES 4)

14 oz [400 g] chicken livers
¼ cup [60 ml] dry sherry
⅞ cup [200 g] butter, diced
1 small onion, finely chopped
¼ cup [50 g] clarified butter
Salt and black pepper

METHOD—Remove any sinews still attached to the livers, wash them, and pat dry. Marinate in the dry sherry at least half an hour.

Melt 2 Tbsp of the butter in a skillet over medium heat, add the onion, and cook about 5 minutes, or until translucent. Add the livers (reserving the marinade), and cook another 5 minutes, or until they are just cooked through. Add the marinade and cook a further 30 seconds. Add the remaining butter and stir until melted, then remove from the heat. Season well with salt and pepper.

Put the liver mixture into a blender or food processor and process to a fine paste. Transfer to a small sterilized storage jar (see p. 251) and cover with clarified butter to seal. Refrigerate at least 2 hours before serving with fresh crusty bread or toast.

DUCK RILLETTE

INGREDIENTS (SERVES 10)

1⅜ cups [300 g] duck fat

2¼ lb [1 kg] duck meat, off the bone,
  skinned and chopped

2 garlic cloves, crushed

2 cloves

1 bay leaf

1 fresh thyme sprig

Salt and black pepper

Rillettes are a type of fatty, spreadable pâté that is very hard to stop eating. Eat with crusty white bread and a pinch of salt.

METHOD—Melt the duck fat in a casserole dish. Add the rest of the ingredients and simmer gently over a very low heat 4 hours. Stir regularly and add a little liquid if necessary. At the end of the cooking time, shred the meat with a fork to make a spreadable paste. Season with salt and pepper and remove the cloves, bay leaf, and thyme. Transfer to sterilized storage jars (see p. 251) and pour over a little duck fat to seal. It will keep in the refrigerator with an unbroken fat layer about a month.

CHORIZO & POTATO EMPANADAS

INGREDIENTS (MAKES APPROX. 12 LARGE ONES)
DOUGH:

4 cups [500 g] all-purpose flour, sieved,
  plus extra for dusting

1 tsp salt

1 tsp sugar

⅞ cup [200 g] butter, diced (alternatively,
  replace half with lard)

2 egg yolks

1 egg, separated, for the glaze

1 Tbsp milk

FILLING:

6 Tbsp vegetable oil

8¾ oz [250 g] chorizo, chopped

2 onions, sliced

½ tsp sugar

1 green bell pepper, seeded and sliced

2 garlic cloves, crushed

½ tsp chili flakes

½ tsp dried thyme

½ tsp dried oregano

1⅛ lb [500 g] boiling potatoes, cut into ⅜ in [1 cm] dice

2 plum tomatoes, skinned and chopped

Salt and black pepper

METHOD—To prepare the dough, combine the sieved flour with the salt and sugar and place on a clean work surface. Make a well in the middle and add the butter. Rub the butter and flour between your fingers until crumbly. Add the yolks and 3 to 4 Tbsp water, and quickly combine all the ingredients into a rough-looking dough. Add more water if necessary; you shouldn't need more than 7 Tbsp [100 ml] in total. Knead it briefly, but don't overwork it. Wrap in plastic wrap and leave to rest 60 minutes in the refrigerator.

Meanwhile, prepare the filling. Heat the oil in a skillet, add the chorizo, and cook over medium heat 3 minutes. Remove and set aside. Reduce the heat to low, add the onions and sugar, and cook 10 minutes. Add the pepper and garlic and cook 15 minutes, stirring regularly. Now add the chili, thyme, oregano, and potatoes. Heat through and add the tomatoes. Cook 10 minutes, or until the potatoes are just tender. Season with salt and pepper. Remove from the heat and stir in the chorizo. Let cool.

Preheat the oven to 400°F [200°C]. Line a baking sheet with baking parchment. Lightly flour the work surface. Remove the dough from the refrigerator and roll it out to a thin sheet, about ¼ in [5 mm] thick. Cut out 4 in [10 cm] diameter circles (use a plate as a template if you like). Place 1 to 2 Tbsp of the filling on each circle and brush the edges with egg white. Fold in half and seal the edges by pressing them firmly together, then crimp the edges with your fingers or a fork. Whisk the egg yolk with the milk and brush the empanadas with this mixture. Transfer to the baking sheet and cook in the oven 25 minutes, or until golden. Remove from the oven and let cool slightly.

BRIK

WITH ANCHOVY & EGG FILLING

INGREDIENTS (MAKES 4)

16 canned anchovy fillets, drained

7 Tbsp [100 ml] milk

2 Tbsp olive oil

1 onion, chopped

1 Tbsp capers, coarsely chopped

4 tsp fresh flat-leaf parsley, chopped

4 sheets malsouka (also known as warka)
   pastry (alternatively, use filo pastry cut
   into 22 in [5 cm] squares)

4 eggs

1 egg white, lightly beaten

Vegetable oil, for shallow frying

Black pepper

Lemon wedges, to serve

METHOD—Place the anchovy fillets in a bowl and cover with the milk. Leave for 30 minutes to 1 hour to extract some of the saltiness. Drain, then finely chop them.

Heat 1 Tbsp olive oil in a skillet and add the onion. Cook over a gentle heat, stirring regularly, 15 minutes, or until very soft. Add the anchovies and remove the pan from the heat. Add the capers and parsley; season with black pepper.

Working with 1 sheet at a time, fold the edges of each malsouka sheet, which are round, to make a square, put a quarter of the anchovy mixture on one side of the pastry to cover it diagonally, and make a hollow in the mixture. Crack an egg into it. Brush the edges of the dough with egg white and fold the other half of the dough over the filling to make a triangular shape. Press the edges to seal.

Fill a large saucepan about one-third full with vegetable oil. Heat over medium heat, and once the oil is hot, carefully place one pastry at a time into the oil and fry 2 minutes, turning once. Remove and drain on paper towels while cooking the remaining briks. Serve hot with lemon wedges.

WILD MUSHROOM RAGOUT & FRIED POLENTA

A pleasingly simple way of getting the best out of your wild harvest. If picking your own, please make sure you know your varieties. Always consult an expert when in doubt.

INGREDIENTS (SERVES 4)
POLENTA:
  8¾ oz [250 g] quick-cook polenta
  Olive oil or butter, for frying
  Salt and black pepper
MUSHROOM RAGOUT:
  14 oz [400 g] mixed wild mushrooms (such as ceps,
    chanterelles, boletus, pied de mouchon, girolles,
    black trompettes), trimmed
  3 Tbsp olive oil
  2 Tbsp butter
  1 shallot, finely chopped
  2 garlic cloves, finely chopped
  ¼ cup [60 ml] dry white wine
  7 Tbsp [100 ml] heavy cream
  1 handful chopped fresh flat-leaf parsley
  Salt and black pepper

METHOD—Bring a pan of water to a boil and cook the polenta according to the instructions on the packet, usually about 5 minutes. Season with salt and pepper. Line a shallow baking dish or tray with baking parchment and pour in the polenta to about ¾ in [2 cm] deep. Leave to set.

Carefully clean the mushrooms with a brush or damp paper towels (do not use water) and trim the stems. Slice any larger varieties, such as ceps. Heat a little oil and the butter in a large pan over high heat and add the mushrooms. Cook 8 to 10 minutes, or until the liquid has evaporated and they have started to take on some color. Remove from the pan. Add a little more oil, add the shallot and garlic, and cook over low heat 3 minutes. Return the mushrooms to the pan, then increase the heat and pour in the wine. Cook until it evaporates, then add the cream. Season with salt and pepper and add the chopped parsley. Cut the polenta sheet into rectangular pieces and brush them with oil. Heat a ridged grill pan until very hot and cook 2 minutes on each side, or until they develop attractive char marks. Serve with the mushroom ragout.

WILD GARLIC PESTO

Wild garlic can fill an entire wood with its heady aroma. Only collect leaves before the plant is blossoming and sniff for the distinctive garlicky smell.

INGREDIENTS (SERVES 4)

3½ oz [100 g] wild garlic

⅔ cup [50 g] Parmesan cheese, grated

2 Tbsp pine nuts

⅝ cup [150 ml] olive oil

Salt

METHOD—Wash the wild garlic thoroughly and place in a blender or food processor with the grated cheese and pine nuts. Season with salt. Process, slowly adding the oil, until well amalgamated. Serve with pasta.

NETTLE & WILD GARLIC SOUP

Pick carefully and enjoy this very fragrant and tasty soup.

INGREDIENTS (SERVES 6)

5¼ oz [150 g] nettle tops

2¾ oz [75 g] wild garlic leaves

4 Tbsp butter

1 large onion, chopped

1 large mealy potato, diced

4½ cups [1 L] light chicken stock, hot (see p. 245)

Sour cream, to serve

Salt and black pepper

METHOD—Thoroughly wash the nettles and wild garlic leaves. Melt the butter in a large saucepan and add the onion. Cook 10 minutes over low heat, until very soft. Add the nettle tops and wild garlic and let them wilt. Season with salt and pepper. Add the potato and the hot chicken stock. Simmer gently 10 minutes until the leaves are soft—the color should still be a verdant green. Transfer to a blender or food processor and process until smooth. Serve with a dollop of sour cream.

BEACHCOMBERS' SHELLFISH

If you have ever walked on a windswept beach, one sniff of this steaming dish of shellfish will instantly transport you back there. Clams and mussels form the base, but you can of course substitute and vary the shellfish depending on what is available on the beach or at the fishmonger. Little brown shrimp and small crabs work well.

INGREDIENTS (SERVES 4)

2¼ lb [1 kg] small live mussels

1⅛ lb [500 g] fresh palourde clams

8 razor clams

2 shallots, finely chopped

14 Tbsp [200 ml] dry white wine

Bouquet garni (3 fresh thyme sprigs, 5 fresh parsley sprigs, and 2 bay leaves tied together)

4½ Tbsp [60 g] butter

3 Tbsp chopped fresh flat-leaf parsley

Salt and pepper

METHOD—Put all your shellfish in a clean sink full of cold water. Discard anything that still floats after it has had a tap with the back of your knife. Scrape off any large barnacles and pull off and discard the beards (the strings hanging out of the shell).

Put the shallots, wine, bouquet garni, and 4 tsp of the butter in a large saucepan. Bring to a boil over high heat and simmer 5 minutes.

Add the shellfish, season with pepper, and stir vigorously. Cover the pan and cook 2 minutes. Shake the pan. Turn off the heat, and leave to stand, covered, 3 more minutes.

Using a slotted spoon, transfer the mussels and clams to a deep serving dish and cover. Strain the cooking juices through a fine strainer into a clean pan and bring to a boil. Reduce for 2 minutes, then whisk in the remaining butter. Stir in the parsley, season with salt and pepper, and pour the sauce over the shellfish. Serve with crusty bread.

SORREL SOUP

INGREDIENTS (SERVES 4)

3 bunches sorrel

2 Tbsp oil or butter

1 shallot, finely chopped

1 mealy potato, cut into small chunks

2 cups [500 ml] light veal stock, hot (see p. 249, or substitute with chicken stock)

7 Tbsp [100 ml] cream

Salt and black pepper

Sorrel has a sour and refreshing taste. You can harvest it from moist meadows in spring and early summer. The young, tender leaves are best, and are a great addition to salads.

METHOD—Wash the sorrel well and remove the stalks. Heat the oil or butter in a pan, add the shallot, and cook 4 to 5 minutes, until soft, then add the sorrel. Once it has wilted, add the hot stock and potato. Simmer 15 minutes, or until just tender. Transfer to a blender or food processor and process until smooth. Season with salt and pepper, add the cream, and serve immediately.

HARE
WITH SOUR CHERRIES

A wonderful dish to eat in the fall. It's still game, whether you hunt it yourself or forage it from a meat counter.

INGREDIENTS (SERVES 6)

2 saddles of hare

6 Tbsp [80 g] clarified butter

4 shallots, finely chopped

14 Tbsp [200 ml] robust dry red wine

4 fresh thyme sprigs

14 Tbsp [200 ml] vegetable stock (optional)

14 oz [400 g] bottled sour cherries

⅓ cup [80 ml] cherry juice, plus 2 Tbsp

1 Tbsp flour

Salt and black pepper

METHOD—Preheat the oven to 400°F [200°C]. Pat the hare dry with paper towels and season it with salt and pepper.

Heat the butter in a large casserole dish, add the hare and cook, turning regularly, until lightly browned on all sides. Remove and set aside. Add the shallots and cook 4 to 5 minutes, or until softened. Add the wine and deglaze the pan, stirring to dissolve any sediment on the bottom, before returning the hare to the pan. Add the thyme, cover, and transfer to the oven. Cook about 45 minutes, basting regularly. If there is too little liquid in the casserole, add a little hot water or stock. After 20 minutes, add the cherries and the cherry juice. After another 20 minutes, remove the hare (which should by now fall off the bone easily), and set aside, covered with aluminum foil, to rest 5 minutes. Return the casserole dish to the hob. Mix the flour with 2 Tbsp cherry juice, add to the casserole, and bring to a boil, stirring, to thicken the sauce. Season with salt and pepper. Cut the meat into slices and serve with the cherry sauce and spätzle or thick pasta, such as pappardelle.

HUNTER'S PHEASANT STEW

INGREDIENTS (SERVES 4)

2 young pheasants, plucked and gutted

Juice of 1 lemon

6 Tbsp [80 g] butter

3½ oz [100 g] pearl or pickling onions, peeled

1 cup [250 ml] dry white wine, such as Riesling

7 Tbsp [100 ml] chicken stock (optional)

3½ oz [100 g] lean bacon, diced

8¾ oz [250 g] chanterelle mushrooms, trimmed and cleaned

1 cup [250 ml] cream

4 tsp fresh flat-leaf parsley, leaves chopped

Salt and black pepper

METHOD—If you're hunting your own birds, you'll need to gut, pluck, and remove the tendons. Regardless, singe the pheasants over an open flame to remove any remaining feathers and stubble. Clean inside and out with damp paper towels, rub with a little lemon juice, and season inside and out with salt and pepper. Cut each bird into 4 pieces.

Melt most of the butter in a casserole dish over medium heat. Add the pheasants and onions and cook until the fowl are lightly browned, about 5 minutes. Add the wine, cover, and simmer gently 30 minutes. Top up with a little stock from time to time if necessary.

Melt a little more butter in another pan and add the bacon and the mushrooms. Cook 5 minutes over high heat, until lightly browned. Remove and transfer to the casserole. Add the cream and cook 1 minute. Add the parsley and season with salt and pepper. Serve hot.

SPIT-ROAST RABBIT

Absolute back-to-nature simplicity. It is possible to spit-roast a rabbit over a campfire, but in practice it is hard to get good results—basting over open flames is hazardous, and not basting gives a rather dry result.

INGREDIENTS (SERVES 2)

1 rabbit, gutted and skinned

12 bacon rashers

Salt and black pepper

MARINADE:

3 garlic cloves, finely chopped

3 fresh rosemary sprigs

1 fresh thyme sprig

2 fresh sage sprigs

2 bay leaves

10 black peppercorns

Juice of 1 lemon

1¼ cups [300 ml] olive oil

METHOD—Put the rabbit in a tight-fitting container or a sealable plastic bag. Combine all the ingredients for the marinade and pour over the rabbit. Marinate at least 1 hour in the refrigerator.

Heat your barbecue until it is very hot and ready to cook over (see p. 266). Remove the rabbit from the marinade. Strain the marinade liquid and reserve it. Season the rabbit with salt and pepper, wrap it in the bacon, and tie it tightly with kitchen string. Insert a spit though the rabbit's neck so that it comes out the other end. Attach the hind legs tightly around the spit and secure the rabbit with kitchen string, so that it won't come off when rotating the spit.

Set the spit up over the barbecue. Roast the rabbit over hot coals, rotating the spit, about 30 minutes, or until it is nicely browned and the flesh is white. Baste it regularly with the reserved marinade (mind the flare-ups) to keep the meat from drying out.

Once cooked, remove from the heat and let the rabbit rest on its spit 15 minutes. Carefully remove from the spit, remove the string, and cut into pieces. Season with salt and pepper before serving. Serve with something juicy; mashed potatoes, perhaps.

SWEET & SOUR WILD BOAR

INGREDIENTS (SERVES 6)

3 oz [80 g] prunes

3 oz [80 g] raisins

3 Tbsp olive oil

3 oz [80 g] bacon, diced

6 wild boar loin chops (about 1⅔ lb [750 g])

3 Tbsp red wine vinegar

1 Tbsp sugar

3 oz [80 g] dark chocolate, grated

4 bay leaves

3 juniper berries

Pinch of ground cinnamon

1 Tbsp flour

7 Tbsp [100 ml] red wine

Salt

A dish for the hunting season. If you don't hunt or have a good local butcher who sells boar, you can replace it with pork or beef. A different flavor, but good nonetheless.

METHOD—Cover the prunes and raisins in hot water and leave to soak 30 minutes. Heat the oil in a casserole dish and add the bacon. Fry 3 to 4 minutes, until it starts to turn golden. Add the meat and brown it on both sides. Season with salt, cover, and cook over low heat 10 minutes.

For the sauce, put the vinegar in a separate pan and heat gently with the sugar, chocolate, bay leaves, juniper berries, and cinnamon, stirring frequently. Make sure the chocolate is completely dissolved.

Drain the prunes and raisins and add them both to the vinegar sauce. Stir the flour into the red wine. Increase the heat under the casserole dish and add the flour and red wine mixture, then cook it for a minute or two before adding the vinegar sauce. Remove the casserole from the heat now, then cover and leave to rest for 10 minutes before serving.

SAMPHIRE, POACHED EGGS & FRIED PARMA HAM

Samphire, also known as glasswort, can be found all around the world in tidal areas. It looks like a seaweed (but it isn't), and it has a great salty flavor. You can eat young samphire raw. It is delicious simply boiled and tossed in butter or as an accompaniment to fish. My favorite, however, is this preparation with bacon and eggs.

INGREDIENTS (SERVES 4)

1¾ lb [800 g] young samphire tips

Butter, to taste

4 eggs

3 Tbsp white wine vinegar

Oil, for frying

3 oz [80 g] Parma ham, sliced

Black pepper

METHOD—Bring a pan of unsalted water to a boil. Add the samphire and simmer 2 minutes. Remove, drain, and return to the pan with a little butter and season with pepper. Toss well, cover, and set aside.

To poach the eggs, place a pan with 6½ cups [1.5 L] water over the heat and add the vinegar to the water. When the water boils, reduce the heat to a simmer, and make a whirlpool in the water with a spoon. Crack 1 egg into a ladle and slide it quickly into the still-swirling water. Cook until the white has completely set, but the yolk is still runny—about 3 minutes. Remove with a slotted spoon and drain on paper towels while you poach the remaining eggs.

Heat a little oil in a skillet over medium heat. Add the Parma ham and fry about 1 minute on each side, until crisp.

To serve, make a bed of samphire on each plate, followed by an egg and a piece of Parma ham.

RANCH-STYLE EGGS

A.K.A. *huevos rancheros.* Darn fine eggs.

INGREDIENTS (SERVES 2)

Olive oil, for frying

½ large onion, chopped

1 garlic clove, finely chopped

1 x 14 oz [400 g] can whole tomatoes

1 mild green chili, finely diced

2 Tbsp fresh cilantro leaves, chopped (optional)

4 corn tortillas

Butter, for frying

4 eggs

Salt and black pepper

Refried beans and queso fresco, or other soft white
cheese, to serve (optional)

METHOD—Place a large skillet over medium heat, add a little olive oil, and cook the onion until softened. When the onion is soft, add the garlic. When the garlic has softened, break the tomatoes up with your fingers and add them to the pan. Add the green chili. Season with salt and pepper. Bring to a simmer, reduce the heat to low, and cook gently 10 minutes. Just before serving, stir in half the cilantro, if using.

Meanwhile, heat a little olive oil in a large skillet on medium-high heat, coating the pan with the oil. One by one (or more if your pan is big enough) heat the tortillas in the pan for a minute or two on each side, until they are heated through and softened, and pockets of air bubble up inside them. Transfer the cooked tortillas to a dish and keep warm. Using the same pan, add a little butter and fry the eggs sunny side-up.

To serve, place an egg on top of each tortilla, allowing 2 per serving, and spoon the sauce around the eggs. Top with more sauce, and sprinkle with the remaining cilantro, if using.

Serve with refried beans and a little queso fresco on the side, if you can find some at your local deli.

PHO BO

Pho is Vietnam's national dish, obsession, subject of poetry, and often described as the "soul of the nation." Served by street vendors, it is eaten for breakfast, lunch, and dinner and is a great restorative. Pho Bo (with beef)—originally from Saigon—is my favorite. Serve with clouds of steam, straight from the pot.

INGREDIENTS (SERVES 6)
STOCK:

4 tsp fresh ginger root

2 shallots

3 star anise seeds

1 pod black cardamom (or substitute with more
    star anise)

1 x 1¼ in [3 cm] cinnamon stick

1⅓ lb [600 g] raw beef bones

3 cloves

2 Tbsp fish sauce

8¾ oz [250 g] beef rump or shoulder

Salt

PHO:

3½ oz [100 g] beef fillet, sliced very thinly

1⅓ lb [600 g] fresh pho rice noodles, or 14 oz [400 g]
    dried rice noodles

2¼ oz [60 g] each of fresh mint, cilantro, Vietnamese
    (saw-tooth) cilantro (or use double the quantity
    of ordinary cilantro)

2 scallions, sliced

2 red chilies, finely chopped

2 limes, cut into quarters

METHOD—Preheat the grill to its highest setting. Grill the ginger and shallots (unpeeled) until blackened on the outside. Alternatively, if you have a gas stove, char them directly over an open flame. Cut, peel or wash away the blackened outer layers. Roughly crush the star anise and cardamom, if using, and put them in a piece of muslin with the cinnamon and cloves, then tie securely. Mix the sliced raw beef fillet with a little of the grilled ginger. Rinse the beef bones and put them in a large pan with 3 qt [3 L] cold water. Bring to a boil and cook briskly, skimming regularly, about 10 minutes. Add the ginger and shallots, spices, fish sauce, and beef rump, reduce the heat and simmer gently about 3 hours.

Remove the spices and bones and discard them. Remove the beef rump and set it aside to drain and dry. Skim again if necessary and season if needed. Keep the stock hot, but be careful not to let it reduce too much.

Slice some of the rump into bite-size pieces. If using fresh rice noodles, blanch them in boiling water 2 seconds. If using dried noodles, cook according to the instructions on the packet. Put the noodles in the serving bowls. Arrange the cooked and raw meat and the herbs on top and pour over the stock to cover (if you do not like your meat too rare, blanch it in the stock 1 to 2 minutes first). Top with the scallions and chilies and serve with fresh lime wedges on the side.

GARLIC SALAMI OMELETTE
WITH PICKLE JUICE SHOT

This omelette is quick and dirty food, perfect for a morning where your need is great but your motor skills may be impaired. You will need the rindless Jewish soft garlic sausage that comes in plastic. It cooks to an agreeably garish pink. Pickle juice (in other words, the liquid from the pickle jar) is a Polish hangover cure and works because of the large dose of salt and sugar, and of course water.

INGREDIENTS (SERVES 2)

4 eggs

1 Tbsp neutral-flavored oil

12 slices soft garlic salami

Salt and black pepper

Pickle juice, to serve

METHOD—Lightly beat the eggs together and season with salt and pepper.

Heat the oil in a skillet large enough to hold all the sausage in one layer. Once hot, add the salami and fry briefly on both sides.

Pour the eggs into the pan around the salami so that it is not covered, but remains like islands of meat in the sea of eggs. Cook 3 to 4 minutes, or until the eggs are just set, and serve with a small shot of pickle juice.

KEDGEREE

INGREDIENTS (SERVES 6)

4 lb [1.8 kg] smoked haddock

2 bay leaves

2 cloves

6 black peppercorns

1⅛ cup [250 g] butter

15¾ oz [450 g] basmati rice

2 onions, chopped

8 eggs, hard-boiled

3 tsp ground cumin

2 tsp ground coriander

2 tsp turmeric

4 tsp fresh flat-leaf parsley, chopped

2 lemons, cut into wedges

METHOD—Place the fish in a pan, cover with cold water, add the bay leaves, cloves, and peppercorns, and heat gently until the water is just beginning to boil. Turn off the heat and remove the fish, reserving the water.

Melt 1½ Tbsp of the butter in a large pan with a lid, add the rice, and stir until evenly coated and opaque. Add the fish-cooking liquid so it is twice the volume of the rice.

Bring the rice pan to a boil and simmer 3 minutes, or until the level of water has fallen just below the level of rice. Do not stir at any point. Cover the pan with a clean dish towel, making sure it does not hang over onto the stove, and press the lid on tightly. Cook 15 minutes over the lowest possible heat (use a heat diffuser if you have one). Remove the dish towel and lid and gently fluff up the rice with a wooden spoon.

While the rice cooks, melt 4 Tbsp butter in another pan and cook the onions over low heat 15 minutes, or until soft. Flake the fish into large pieces and remove every scrap of skin and bone. Shell the hard-boiled eggs and quarter them. When the rice and the onions are ready, add the rest of the butter to the onions, let it melt, add the spices, and cook gently 2 to 3 minutes. Stir them into the rice. Finally, add the fish, eggs, and parsley to the rice and serve with lemon wedges.

PIMPED
INSTANT NOODLES

INGREDIENTS (SERVES 1)

1 packet instant noodles

HOT PIMPING:

1 fresh mild red chili, finely shredded

Large pinch dried chili flakes or 1 tsp chili oil, or both

3 scallions, or ½ red onion, finely chopped

Juice of ½ lime

MEAT PIMPING:

Handful mushrooms, sliced

Handful cooked pork or beef, cut into thin strips

1 tsp dark soy sauce

1 tsp neutral-flavored oil

2 in [5 cm] fresh ginger root, finely chopped

3 scallions, or ½ red onion, finely chopped

1 garlic clove, chopped

HEALTHY PIMPING:

Handful cooked shrimps

Handful fresh cilantro, chopped

3 scallions, or ½ red onion, finely chopped

Handful bean sprouts

Complex activities can be somewhat challenging when you're hungover, and shortcuts to wellness may be the order of the day. Instant noodles give you liquid and are just fine, but pimped noodles are better. Just choose your pimping style.

METHOD—For the hot pimping, add the dried chili (if using) to the liquid when it reaches a boil. Serve and top with the other ingredients.

For the meat pimping, put the mushrooms and meat together in a small bowl and stir in the soy sauce. Heat a wok or skillet with the oil until it is very hot, add the meat and mushrooms, and fry 2 minutes. Now add the ginger, scallions, and garlic and fry a further minute. Add to your bowl of cooked noodles.

For the healthy pimping, bring the liquid to the boil. Add the shrimp along with the noodles. Serve topped with the cilantro, scallions, and bean sprouts.

PRAIRIE OYSTER

"It is the Worcestershire sauce that gives it its color. The raw egg makes it nutritious. The red pepper gives it its bite. Gentlemen have told me they have found it extremely invigorating after a late evening."

—P. G. Wodehouse, *Jeeves Takes Charge* (1916)

INGREDIENTS (SERVES 1)

1 egg

2 dashes Worcestershire sauce

1 dash hot sauce, such as Tabasco

Salt and black pepper

METHOD—Break the egg into a glass, keeping the yolk intact. Add the Worcestershire sauce and the hot sauce and sprinkle with salt and pepper. Down in one gulp.

EGGS BENEDICT

INGREDIENTS (SERVES 6)

3 Tbsp white wine vinegar

4 eggs

8 rashers bacon

2 English muffins, sliced in half and toasted

Butter, for spreading

HOLLANDAISE SAUCE:

⅞ cup [200 g] butter

3 egg yolks

2 tsp lemon juice

Salt and cayenne pepper

METHOD—Start by making the hollandaise. Melt the butter in a saucepan and leave 1 minute. Remove the white froth on the surface. Carefully pour the butter into a pitcher, leaving the white residue behind.

Bring a pan of water to a boil, then reduce the heat and let it simmer. Put the egg yolks in a heatproof bowl set over a pan of barely simmering water. Make sure the base of the bowl doesn't touch the water. Add 4 tsp water, a pinch of salt, and a pinch of cayenne pepper to the eggs and whisk about 5 minutes until you have a thick and foamy consistency. Remove from the pan and add the warm (but not hot) butter, little by little. Whisk until well emulsified. Remove the pan from the heat and keep the sauce warm over it while poaching the eggs. Whisk in some lemon juice just before serving.

Place a pan containing 6½ cups [1.5 L] water over the heat and add the vinegar. When the water boils, reduce to a simmer, and make a whirlpool in the water with a spoon. Crack 1 egg into a ladle and slide it quickly into the still-swirling water. Cook until the white has set completely but the yolk is still runny—about 3 minutes. Place on paper towels to drain and poach the remaining eggs. Meanwhile, pan-fry the bacon rashers 4 minutes on each side, or until crisp. Toast the muffins, butter them, and place half the bacon on each one, a poached egg on top, and pour over the hollandaise sauce.

PANCAKE SOUP

INGREDIENTS (SERVES 2)

⅞ cup [100 g] flour

½ tsp salt

14 Tbsp [200 ml] milk

1 egg

Vegetable oil, for frying

2½ cups [600 ml] good-quality beef stock (see p. 245)

Bunch fresh chives, chopped

An Austrian staple. To the best of my knowledge, this is not considered breakfast in those parts, but it does work wonders after a night out.

METHOD—Make the pancake batter by putting the flour, salt, milk, and egg in a bowl and whisking together until smooth. Heat a little oil in a nonstick skillet. When the pan is very hot, add a ladle of batter and swirl it around the pan. Cook until golden, about 30 seconds to 1 minute on each side. Remove from the pan and let cool.

Roll each pancake up and slice thinly to make pasta-like strips and place into 2 soup bowls. Pour the very hot stock over them immediately and add the chives to serve.

CHURROS
HOT CHOCOLATE
& BRANDY

INGREDIENTS (SERVES 4)

HOT CHOCOLATE:

7 Tbsp [100 ml] milk

14 Tbsp [200 ml] heavy cream

1 vanilla pod, seeds scraped out

1 cinnamon stick

8¾ oz [250 g] good-quality dark chocolate, grated

CHURROS:

3 Tbsp vegetable oil or butter, cut into pieces

2 cups [250 g] self-rising flour, sifted

½ tsp salt

Vegetable oil, for deep-frying

DUSTING:

1 Tbsp ground cinnamon

3 Tbsp sugar

METHOD—For the churros dough, bring 1¼ cups [300 ml] water to a boil and add the oil (or butter until it melts). In a mixing bowl, combine the flour and salt. Make a well and pour in the hot water. Mix continuously until you achieve a smooth mixture without lumps. Leave to rest 20 minutes.

Gently heat the milk, cream, vanilla pod and seeds, and cinnamon in a pan. When it starts to boil, remove from the heat and set aside to infuse 10 minutes. Remove the vanilla pod and the cinnamon stick and reheat until on the verge of boiling. Remove from the heat once more and add the chocolate. Stir constantly until the chocolate has melted and the texture is smooth.

Heat the oil for deep-frying in a deep pan or a deep-fat fryer to 325°F [170°C]. Fill a piping bag with a star-shaped nozzle with the churros batter and carefully pipe 4 in [10 cm] pieces of the dough directly into the fryer, cutting off each one with scissors. Cook about 5 minutes, or until golden brown. Fry them in batches—don't overcrowd the pan, as they stick together easily. Remove and drain on paper towels. Stir together the cinnamon and sugar for dusting on a plate and dust the churros with the mixture.

Serve the churros immediately with the hot chocolate and a glass of brandy.

ORAL REHYDRATION SOLUTION

Overindulged? The best way to recover is simply to rehydrate yourself quickly and replace your electrolytes. The banana is a great addition as it's easy on a delicate stomach, and full of potassium. It isn't fancy, but it works.

INGREDIENTS (SERVES 1)

½ tsp baking soda

1 tsp salt

8 tsp sugar

1 banana (optional)

METHOD—Boil 4½ cups [1 L] water and let cool a little. Stir the baking soda, salt, and sugar into the water until they dissolve. Chill in the refrigerator. Drink plenty of it, and eat a banana if you can.

PRESERVED FROM SCRATCH

GRAVADLAX

INGREDIENTS (SERVES 8)

2 large bunches fresh dill, finely chopped

6¼ oz [175 g] sea salt

1¾ cups [350 g] superfine sugar

2 Tbsp ground black pepper

1 wild salmon, prepared as 2 whole boned fillets,
   5 to 6 lb [2.2 to 2.8 k] in total

METHOD—Mix together the chopped dill, salt, sugar, and pepper. Lay out a large piece of aluminum foil and put about one-quarter of the curing mixture on it, then place a fillet, skin-side down, on top of it. Cover with half the mixture. Place the other fillet, skin-side up, on top of the first fillet and cover it with the remaining quarter of the mixture. If you have a smaller or larger fish, reduce or expand the quantities for the curing mixture accordingly. The ratio of sugar to salt is always 2:1. Wrap the fillets so that the resulting package is quite tight and the edges are tucked under.

Put the foil package in a large plastic container so that it can lie flat, and place a weight on top—a couple of cans, perhaps—ensuring that the weight is fairly evenly dispersed. Place in the refrigerator. Turn the package every day for 5 to 7 days.

To serve, remove from the refrigerator and brush off any remaining cure. Slice each fillet thinly at an angle of about 30°, skin-side down. Cut the slices relatively thick, otherwise they may tear, and use a very sharp knife.

CONFIT DUCK

Duck prepared in this ancient way tastes more duck-like; almost as though, after the cooking, you are left with the essence of duck.

INGREDIENTS (SERVES 4)

4 duck legs
8 Tbsp salt
4 garlic cloves, sliced
1 bunch fresh thyme
4 dried bay leaves, crumbled
2¼ lb [1 kg] duck fat
1 tsp black pepper

METHOD—Using a small sharp knife, cut through the fat in a circle shape around the end of each thigh bone. This will allow the meat and skin to rise up during cooking.

Choose a dish deep enough to hold all the legs, and into which they will fit snugly. Line it with plastic wrap and place the duck legs inside. Rub them thoroughly with the salt, pepper, garlic, thyme, and bay leaves. Wrap them in the plastic wrap and refrigerate for 48 hours, turning the legs after 24 hours.

Preheat the oven to 200°F [100°C]. Put the duck fat in an ovenproof dish with 3 Tbsp water and place in the oven to heat through. You will need enough fat to just cover the duck legs. The water will prevent the duck from becoming too dark.

While the fat is heating, unwrap the duck legs and brush off all the salt, herbs, and garlic marinade.

When the fat is "shivering"—just before it boils—add the legs, carefully cover the dish with foil (the fat will be extremely hot), and cook about 3 hours. Depending on your duck and your preference, you may adjust the cooking time. I like my confit to be almost falling off the bone. Make sure the fat does not boil; it should be just below boiling point during the cooking.

Once they are cooked, place a wire rack over a plate and very carefully transfer the legs onto the rack. They will be very fragile, so take your time. While the duck legs rest, clarify the fat by ladling it through a fine sieve into a bowl, being careful not to take any of the brown duck juices that will have collected under the fat.

Put a ladle of the strained fat in a glazed earthenware pot with a lid or glass storage jar that is large enough to hold all the legs and fat. Put the container in the refrigerator for 15 minutes, or until the fat has solidified. Carefully place the duck legs in the container so that they do not touch the sides, and pour in the remaining clarified fat. Let it settle, then shake the jar very gently to help release any air pockets. Cover with the lid and place in the refrigerator until the fat solidifies, then press a piece of baking parchment into the top of the jar and seal with the lid. If you sterilize your container (see p. 251), the confit will keep refrigerated for several months.

SALT BEEF

INGREDIENTS (SERVES 8)

4½ lb [2 kg] beef brisket, rolled

BRINE:

1⅔ lb [750 g] rock salt

1¼ cup [250 g] sugar

2¼ Tbsp Prague powder #1
  (a curing salt containing sodium nitrite)

4 garlic cloves

4 bay leaves

2 whole cloves

2 allspice berries

2 star anise

3 fresh thyme sprigs

COOKING:

2 large onions, quartered

3 carrots, coarsely chopped

2 celery stalks, coarsely chopped

2 bay leaves

2 fresh parsley sprigs

2 garlic cloves

METHOD—Combine the ingredients for the brine with 5¼ qt [5 L] water in a large pan and bring to a boil. Stir occasionally to dissolve the salt and sugar. Reduce the heat and simmer 5 minutes, then remove from the heat and let cool completely.

Put the rolled brisket, tied with kitchen string, in a nonmetallic container or strong, sealable plastic bag. Pour over the cold brine, and make sure the meat is completely covered. Cover and put in the refrigerator. Leave to sit 7 to 10 days, turning the meat every day.

After the brining, discard the liquid, place the meat in another container, and cover with fresh water. Leave in the refrigerator another 24 hours to extract some of the excess salt.

The next day, place the meat in a large casserole dish and add the onions, carrots, celery, bay leaves, parsley, and garlic. Cover with cold water and bring to a boil. Reduce the heat and let simmer 2½ hours, or until the meat is very tender. Top up with water regularly. Serve hot as a pot-roast, or cold in slices on rye bread with pickles.

HOMEMADE BACON

Bacon is incredibly easy to make at home—
all you need is some curing salt and a
working refrigerator. Carving a slab off your
own side of bacon is surprisingly satisfying,
and it impresses your friends.

INGREDIENTS (MAKES ABOUT 3½ LB [1.6 KG])

- 2 oz [60 g] crystal or rock salt
- 1 tsp Prague powder #1 (a curing salt containing
  sodium nitrite)
- 1 Tbsp sugar
- 1 tsp ground black pepper
- 4½ lb [2 kg] pork belly, thin end

METHOD—Mix together the salt, Prague powder, sugar,
and black pepper. Put your pork belly on a clean work
surface and rub it with 4 tsp of the mixture. Put it in a
large sealable plastic bag or plastic box with a lid. Put
this in your refrigerator.

Turn every day for 5 days. You now have genuine
bacon. Wash off any remaining curing mixture and dry
your bacon with a clean cloth. Wrap it in muslin and
attach a string around it. Hang it up somewhere to let it
dry for a day. Afterward, put it in the refrigerator, where
it will keep for several weeks. You can extend its shelf-
life by curing it for longer (up to 2 weeks), but it will also
get saltier. If it is too salty for your taste, you can put the
bacon in a bowl of cold clean water for a couple of hours
before using.

BRESAOLA

To make the Italian cured beef, bresaola, at home, you need a cool, moist place to hang your meat—a garage or cellar, for example. It is really easy to make, but you must check in on your meat regularly to avoid disappointment.

INGREDIENTS (MAKES ABOUT 2¼ LB [1 KG])

2½ lb [1.3 kg] beef topside, in one piece

8 Tbsp salt

8 Tbsp sugar

1 tsp Prague powder #2
  (a curing salt containing sodium nitrite)

2 tsp ground black pepper

2 tsp ground juniper

3 tsp dried rosemary

2 dried bay leaves, broken into pieces

METHOD—First, trim any fat and skin off your beef. Now make the salt cure by mixing together all the remaining ingredients. Rub half the mixture onto the meat and put it in a plastic container with a lid in the refrigerator. Turn it once a day for a week. After a week, take the meat and container out of the refrigerator. Rinse out the container and pat the meat dry with a clean cloth. Cover the meat with the remaining cure and put it back in the refrigerator. Continue turning it every day for another week.

After 2 weeks, wash off any remaining cure and pat it dry with a cloth. Tie it up with string in a series of butcher's knots (see p. 273) and hang in a cool, moist, well ventilated place. Check the humidity level, it needs to be between 60 to 70 percent. The bresaola will be ready once it has lost 25 to 30 percent of its weight, in about 3 weeks.

Check it regularly, daily if possible. Smell it. If it smells like rotting meat, sadly, it is, and you have to trash it. White mold should appear; that is fine. Black spots, on the other hand, should be removed quickly with a cloth soaked in a little vinegar.

Serve it sliced very thinly, as the Italians do, with just a drizzle of olive oil and a squeeze of lemon juice.

PRESERVED LEMONS

The chopped peel of preserved lemons is a standard in North African cuisine, but it's also very versatile. Try it mixed with parsley, crushed garlic, herbs, and butter to serve with fried fish, for example. Usually only the peel is used, but the pulp also works wonders in a Bloody Mary.

INGREDIENTS (MAKES 1 × 2¼ LB [1 KG] JAR)

- 12 unwaxed lemons
- 8¾ oz [250 g] coarse sea salt
- 2 bay leaves (optional)
- 10 black peppercorns (optional)
- 1 cinnamon stick (optional)

METHOD—Wash the lemons and scrub them with a brush. Dry them with a clean dish towel. Cut the lemons lengthwise into quarters to within ⅜ in [1 cm] of the stem—don't cut all the way through. The segments should be attached to each other at the base.

Gently prize open the lemons and sprinkle 1 to 2 tsp of salt into each one. Now fill a glass storage jar with a nonmetallic lid with the lemons, open side facing downward. Add a generous amount of salt after each layer of lemons (about 1 Tbsp salt per lemon). Add the spices, if using. Press down the lemons tightly to release their juices. If there is not enough juice to cover them all, add some extra lemon juice or boiling water.

Cover with a lid and leave to macerate at room temperature at least 4 weeks. Before using, wash the lemon pieces with water to drain them of the excess salt.

SMOKED HAM HOCK

Smoked ham hock is extremely moreish. The meat's intense smoky-porky flavor makes it a great partner for dishes made with legumes. It is also pretty straightforward to make. Ideally, you should buy a smoker (good, inexpensive smokers are easy to find online), although you can also use a barbecue if it has a lid.

INGREDIENTS (MAKES 2)

3½ oz [100 g] salt

½ cup [100 g] sugar

1 Tbsp Prague powder #1 (a curing salt containing sodium nitrite)

½ Tbsp ground black pepper

2 bay leaves

2 ham hocks, about 1⅔ lb [750 g] each

1⅛ lb [500 g] hickory chips

METHOD—Bring 5¼ qt [5 L] water to a boil and turn off the heat. Add all the ingredients except the hocks and hickory chips and stir until completely dissolved. Cool to room temperature, then transfer to a large, sealable plastic container. Add the hocks, seal, and place in the refrigerator. Ensure the hocks are completely submerged in the brine; use a saucer or plate as a weight if they are misbehaving. Refrigerate for 4 days. Use it as you would smoked bacon. I like to eat it instead of bacon for breakfast, and as an addition to soups, for example in Pea & Ham Hock Soup (see p. 95). It'll keep in the refrigerator for up to a week in an airtight container.

Remove the hocks from the brine and soak them in fresh water 3 hours. Pat them dry and return to the refrigerator until you are going to use them.

Soak the hickory chips in water 1 hour. If using a smoker, set it up according the manufacturer's instructions. Place your soaked chips in the tray, place your hocks on the rack, and smoke 4 to 5 hours, or to taste. If using a barbecue, you need to use a medium (about 450°F [230°C]) indirect heat (see p. 266), with the lid closed. Smoke 4 to 5 hours, or to taste.

PICKLED HERRINGS

INGREDIENTS (SERVES 4)

8 herrings

½ tsp sugar

4 tsp sea salt

MARINADE:

3¾ cups [900 ml] white wine vinegar

2½ cups [500 g] sugar

25 allspice berries

30 black peppercorns

2 bay leaves

2 small carrots, thinly sliced

2 small onions, thinly sliced

Easy to make, with excellent results every time. Just remember that it's paramount that the marinade is completely cold before you pour it over the herring—you do not want to cook them. They are wonderful as part of a *smorgasbord*, or delicious just with a hunk of good bread and a dollop of dill mustard sauce.

METHOD—Ask your fishmonger to scale, gut, and fillet your herrings. It's quite fiddly, but you can of course do this yourself. Put them in a plastic container with a lid. Mix together the sugar and salt and coat them inside and out with the mixture. Put the lid on and place in the refrigerator for 48 hours. If there is any salt left after this time, brush it away.

Put all the marinade ingredients together in a pan and bring to a boil. Let cool completely, then put the herrings and marinade into a sterilized storage jar (see p. 251) or airtight plastic food container. They will keep for about 3 weeks like this.

SAUERKRAUT

INGREDIENTS (MAKES ABOUT 2¼ LB [1 KG])

- 1 white cabbage (about 4½ lb [2 kg])
- Sea salt, for curing
- 3 bay leaves
- 6 juniper berries
- 1 tsp caraway seeds

METHOD—Sterilize a large glass jar or several smaller ones (see p. 251). It is important not to use one with a metal lid, as it would react with the cabbage.

Cut out the core from the cabbage and remove the outer leaves. Using a large knife or a mandolin, finely shred the cabbage. Weigh the shredded cabbage. In a large bowl, mix in ⅓ tsp salt per 3½ oz [100 g] cabbage and knead it with your fists until juices starts to emerge.

Add the bay leaves, juniper, and caraway, and stir well.

Fill your sterilized jar(s) with cabbage in stages, regularly pressing it down. Cover the top with a whole leaf. It should be filled to four-fifths full. Loosely cover the jar with its lid. If using a kilner jar, remove the rubber seal. Brine will quickly begin to form, which should cover the cabbage completely. If it does not, it will rot. If necessary, weight the cabbage down with something sterilized and nonmetallic, or press down regularly with a spoon. Put the jar in a bowl to catch any overflow and leave at room temperature (65 to 68°F [18 to 20°C]) for 3 to 6 days. Once the liquid has stopped flowing, tightly seal it (and attach the rubber seal if there is one), then transfer to a cool place. It is ready after 2 to 3 weeks to use. Unopened, it keeps for up to a year.

PICKLED EGGS

"My boy says he can eat fifty eggs, he can eat fifty eggs."

—Dragline in *Cool Hand Luke* (1967)

INGREDIENTS (MAKES 12)

- 1¾ oz [50 g] salt
- 1 tsp sugar
- 2 tsp caraway or mustard seeds
- 1 tsp black peppercorns
- 2 bay leaves
- Skin of 2 onions
- 12 eggs

METHOD—In a large pan, bring 4½ cups [1 L] water to a boil with the salt, sugar, spices, bay leaves, and onion skin. Stir until all the salt has dissolved and take off the heat.

Prick the egg shells with a pin and boil 10 minutes in the water. Remove and plunge into cold water. Carefully crack the shell of each egg slightly and all over, but do not peel them, and place the eggs in a large glass jar. This will create a marble pattern after the eggs have marinated. Now pour over the cooking water (including all the spices), seal the jar, and leave 2 days in the refrigerator. Serve with mustard and black pepper, with oil and vinegar drizzled over.

MANLY DESSERTS

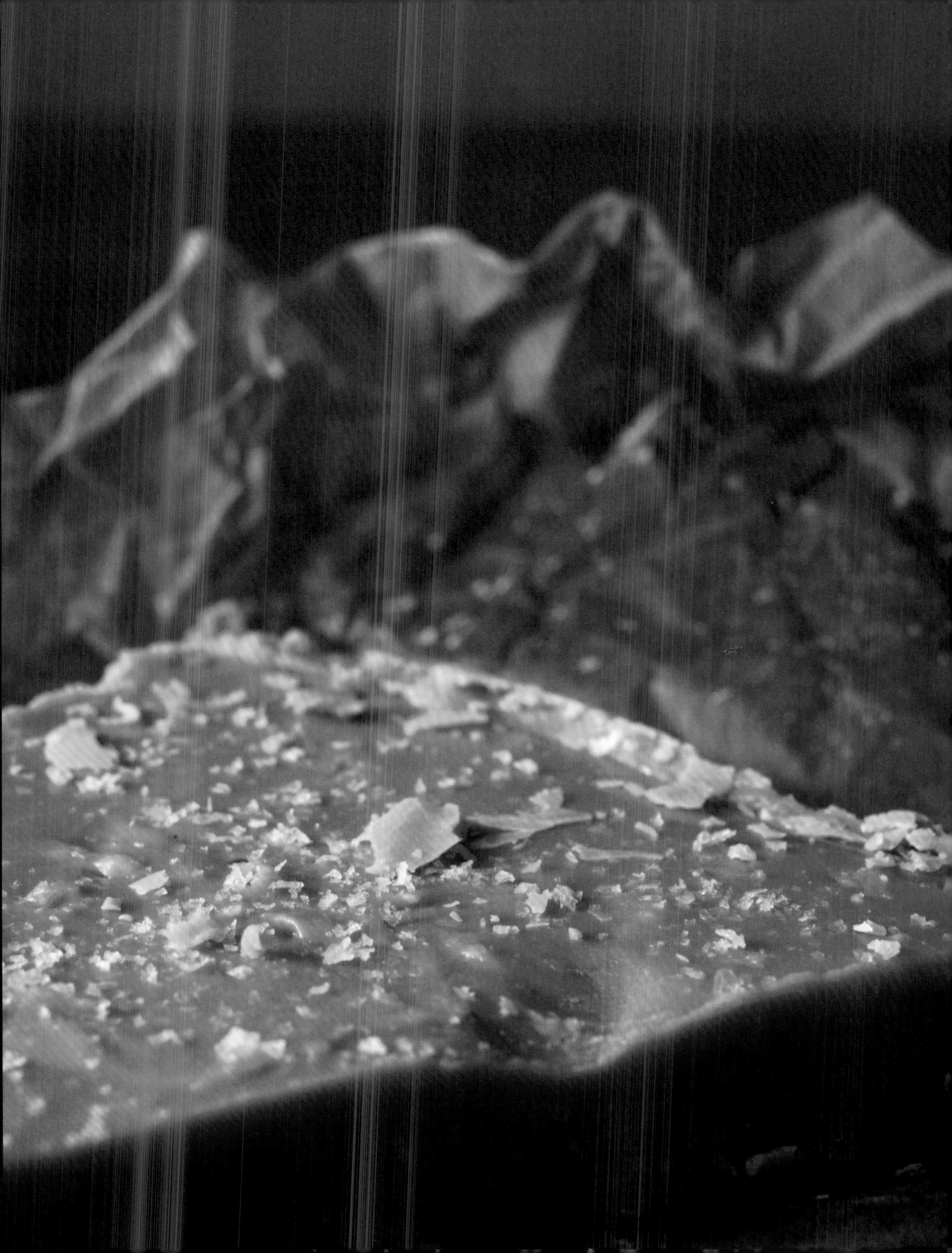

SALTED CARAMEL FUDGE

Perfect emergency rations for an extended hiking trip in the wilderness.

INGREDIENTS (MAKES ABOUT 20 PIECES)

Flavorless oil, for greasing

2¼ cups [450 g] brown sugar

⅔ cup [150 g] butter

⅝ cup [150 ml] milk

1 x 14 oz [400 g] can sweetened condensed milk

½ tsp salt flakes, plus extra for sprinkling

METHOD—Grease an 8 in [20 cm] square tin and line it with baking parchment.

Put the sugar in a nonstick saucepan over medium heat, cook until dissolved, and let it turn very slightly caramelized. Add the butter, milk, and condensed milk and stir continuously with a wooden spoon. Once the butter and sugar have completely melted, bring to a boil and continue to stir for 20 minutes while the mixture boils. It should reach 240°F [115°C], or soft ball stage: if you drop a bit of the mixture into a glass of water it should form a soft ball, but it's easier to use a sugar thermometer instead.

Remove from the heat and continue to beat the mixture with a spoon for 10 minutes, until thickened and slightly grainy, and the glossy shine has gone. Crumble and add the sea salt flakes, stir well, and pour into the prepared tin. Sprinkle a few salt flakes on top, pushing them in a little, so that they stick. Chill the fudge in the refrigerator 6 hours. Remove from the tin and cut into pieces.

UPSIDE-DOWN APPLE TART

This famous tart is the Schrödinger's cat of baking. You just can't be sure what comes out at the end until you see for yourself. Definitely a risk worth taking, so man up.

INGREDIENTS (SERVES 6)

1½ cups [300 g] sugar

1 egg

1¾ cups [350 g] butter, softened

2 cups [250 g] flour, plus extra for dusting

1 Tbsp milk (if necessary)

2¼ lb [1 kg] apples, such as Cox or Braeburn

1 lemon

1 Tbsp vanilla sugar

Salt

METHOD—Mix together ½ cup [100 g] of the sugar, the egg and a pinch of salt and whisk until smooth. Whisk in ⅔ cup [150 g] of the soft butter. Little by little, add the flour, and bring together with your hands until well incorporated into a soft dough. If the mixture is too crumbly, add 1 Tbsp of milk. Shape it into a ball, wrap it in plastic wrap, and chill in the refrigerator at least 2 hours.

Peel, core, and quarter the apples (you might want to prepare a few spare ones, just in case) and sprinkle them with a little lemon juice.

Melt the remaining butter in a tarte tatin tin over medium heat. Once the butter is bubbling, add ¾ cup [150 g] of the sugar. Let it dissolve for a minute and add the apple pieces. They should sit in the mold as tightly as possible in one layer, so add a few more if necessary. Sprinkle the top with the remaining sugar and the vanilla sugar. Cook over gentle heat until the caramel becomes quite dark, but not burned—this takes about 20 minutes. Preheat the oven to 400°F [200°C].

Remove the dough from the refrigerator and roll it out on a lightly floured surface to a circle the same size as the mold, about ¼ in [5 mm] thick. Once the apples have taken on a dark color, take off the heat and cover with the pastry, tucking it in slightly. Don't leave any overhang.

Bake in the oven 20 minutes, then cover with aluminum foil and reduce the heat to 300°F [150°C]. Bake another 10 minutes. Remove from the oven and place on very wet paper towels to stop the caramel cooking any further. After at least 10 minutes—or when ready to serve—put the tin back over the heat 1 minute to melt the bottom, carefully turn out onto a serving dish and serve warm with whipped cream or ice cream.

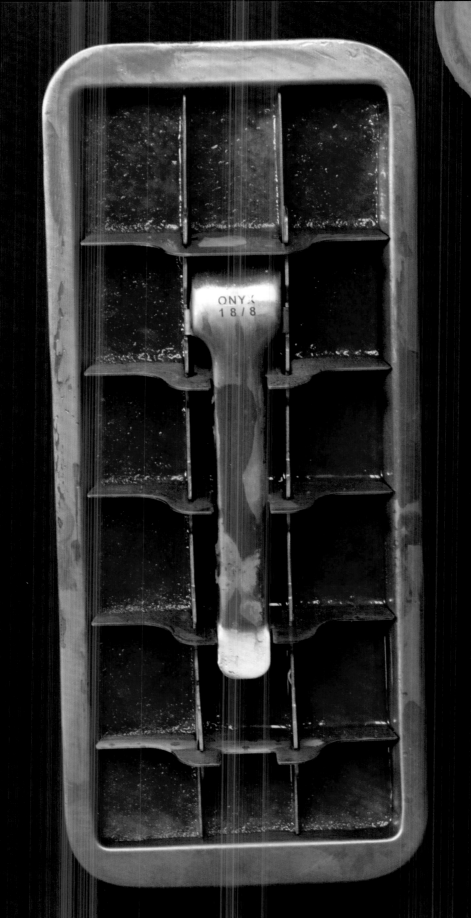

SEA BREEZE SORBET

This is a Sea Breeze cocktail deconstructed as a frozen dessert. All you need is a freezer and a blender, no ice-cream machine required.

INGREDIENTS (SERVES 6)

2 cups [500 ml] cranberry juice

¾ cup [150 g] sugar

1 cup [250 ml] pink grapefruit juice, preferably freshly squeezed

Vodka (optional)

1 egg white (optional; this stabilizes the mixture but unfortunately turns the sorbet garishly pink)

METHOD—Put the cranberry juice and sugar in a saucepan and bring to a boil. Simmer 3 minutes, or until the sugar has completely dissolved, stirring frequently. Remove from the heat and add the grapefruit juice. Cool to room temperature and chill in the refrigerator.

Pour the liquid into 2 ice-cube trays and freeze for at least 8 hours. If you are having frozen vodka with your sorbet, put the vodka in the freezer at the same time, along with some shot glasses. Shortly before serving, remove the trays from the freezer and put 1 batch of sorbet cubes in the food processor, with the egg white, if using. Pulse it, but don't blend it completely, as the ice will continue to melt and you'll end up with liquid shortly thereafter. Tasty, but not a sorbet. Repeat with the remaining ice cubes and place a scoop on each plate. Pour the frozen vodka into the chilled shot glasses and serve alongside the sorbet.

GINGERED
RHUBARB CRUMBLE

===

One of the all-time classic flavor combinations.

===

INGREDIENTS (SERVES 6)

2¼ lb [1 kg] rhubarb

¼ cup [50 g] fresh ginger, grated

¾ cup [150 g] sugar

1 piece lemon or orange zest

1 vanilla pod, split

7 Tbsp [100 ml] white wine

TOPPING:

5 Tbsp [50 g] flour

7 Tbsp [100 g] butter, cubed

1 cup [200 g] brown sugar

3 oz [80 g] ground almonds

⅔ cup [50 g] oats

Pinch of ground cinnamon

Salt

PUDDING:

1 cup [250 ml] heavy cream

1 cup [250 ml] milk

1 vanilla pod, split

3 egg yolks

⅓ cup [60 g] sugar

METHOD—Wash the rhubarb, trimming off the roots. If the rhubarb is old, tear the red skin off in long strips and discard it (this is not necessary for young, tender rhubarb). Cut the rhubarb into ¾ in [2 cm] chunks. Put the rhubarb in a saucepan with the ginger, sugar, lemon, or orange zest and vanilla, and leave to macerate 2 hours.

Add the wine to the rhubarb pan, place over medium heat, and bring to a boil. Simmer 10 minutes. Preheat the oven to 350°F [180°C].

To make the crumble topping, put the flour and butter in a mixing bowl and rub the butter into the flour with your fingers. Add the brown sugar, almonds, oats, and a pinch each of cinnamon and salt. Crumble the mixture between your fingertips.

Remove the vanilla pod and lemon or orange zest and place the cooked rhubarb in the bottom of a baking dish. Sprinkle the crumble mixture evenly on top. Bake in the oven 30 minutes, or until bubbling and golden. Let stand for a few minutes before serving.

Meanwhile, make the pudding. Put the cream and milk in saucepan, scrape the seeds out of the vanilla pod, and add them to the milk, along with the pod. Place over medium heat. In another bowl, whisk together the egg yolks and sugar. Once the milk has come to a boil, remove the vanilla pod. Pour 2 ladles of hot milk into the egg mixture and whisk vigorously. Pour the egg mixture back into the pan with the milk, stirring continuously with a wooden spoon until the mixture starts to thicken and coats the back of the spoon. Remove from the heat and let cool a little. Serve the crumble with the pudding.

CHOCOLATE BROWNIES

INGREDIENTS (SERVES 6)

Butter, for greasing

7 oz [200 g] good-quality dark chocolate (70 percent cocoa solids)

1⅔ cups [200 g] powdered sugar

3 eggs, at room temperature

⅓ cup [40 g] flour, sifted

METHOD—Preheat the oven to 325°F [170°C]. Grease an 8 x 8 in [20 x 20 cm] baking tin and line it with baking parchment, leaving a little overhanging on every side.

Break the chocolate into pieces and melt it in a heatproof bowl set over a pan of barely simmering water. Once the chocolate has melted, remove from the heat and beat in 3 Tbsp lukewarm water, followed by the powdered sugar. Add the eggs one by one, stirring vigorously to ensure a smooth consistency. Stir in the flour.

Pour the batter into the prepared tin and bake in the oven 20 to 25 minutes, or until small cracks appear on the surface. Serve warm with ice cream, or cold alone.

PRUNES IN ARMAGNAC

This is a great end to a meal. Make too many and you'll always have the thrill of discovering a jar when you thought the cupboard was empty.

INGREDIENTS (MAKES 3 LB [1.5 KG])

1⅔ lb [750 g] prunes (preferably Agen prunes with stones)

3¼ cups [750 ml] weak black tea, cooled

2½ cups [300 g] sugar

1 vanilla pod, split (optional)

3 cups [700 ml] Armagnac

METHOD—Soak the prunes in the tea 2 to 3 hours. Next, prepare a syrup: in a saucepan, melt the sugar, add 1¼ cups [300 ml] water, and the vanilla pod, if using, and bring to a boil. Let cool and remove the vanilla.

Sterilize a storage jar (see p. 251). Pat the prunes dry with paper towels and fill the prepared jar with them. Mix the Armagnac with the sugar syrup and pour it over the prunes to cover them. Seal and shake a little. Leave to macerate at least 1 month (but 3 to 4 months is even better). Serve on their own or with ice cream.

BURNED CREAM

Back in the eighteenth century a branding iron was used to burn the cream. Today a cook's blowtorch or hot grill will do the trick.

INGREDIENTS (SERVES 6)

½ vanilla pod

1 cup [250 ml] milk

1 cup [250 ml] heavy cream

4 egg yolks

⅞ cup [100 g] powdered sugar

½ cup [100 g] superfine sugar

METHOD—Preheat the oven to 300°F [150°C]. Boil a kettleful of water. Split open the vanilla pod lengthwise and put it in a saucepan with the milk and cream. Gently bring to a boil over low heat.

Meanwhile, whisk together the egg yolks and powdered sugar. When the creamy milk is hot, add a little of it to the egg mixture, stirring continuously. Pour the egg mixture back into the pan with the milk and continue to stir well for a minute. Strain the liquid through a fine sieve into 6 small ovenproof ramekins and place them in a large baking dish. Pour the hot water into the dish so that it comes almost all the way up the sides of the ramekins. Carefully transfer it to the oven on the lowest shelf and cook 30 to 40 minutes. The top should be firm but still wobbly when touched.

Remove from the bain-marie and let cool (they can also be left for a day in the refrigerator, covered with plastic wrap). About 1 hour before serving, sprinkle the superfine sugar on the surface of each pudding and place for 2 to 3 minutes under a very hot grill until all the sugar has caramelized. If you have a blowtorch, use that—it only takes seconds. Take care while doing this, as the caramel should be dark, but not too deeply burned. Chill 1 hour before serving.

PEARS IN RED WINE

This is a fabulous dessert. Classically served on its own, it also goes very well with walnut ice cream or a slab of blue cheese.

INGREDIENTS (SERVES 6)

6 pears, such as Williams or Comice

¾ cup [150 g] sugar

3¼ cups [750 ml] good, dry red wine, such as Côtes du Rhône

1 cinnamon stick

2 vanilla pods, split

6 black peppercorns

Zest of 1 lemon

METHOD—Peel the pears, leaving the stem on. Reserve the peel.

Put the sugar in a large, heavy-based pan and heat over medium heat until caramelized to a dark amber color. Add the wine, standing well back. Reduce the heat. Once the caramel has dissolved, add the cinnamon, vanilla, peppercorns, lemon zest, and pear peelings. Simmer 20 minutes. Add the pears and simmer another 10 minutes.

Transfer the pears to a bowl and strain the cooking liquid onto them. Leave to macerate at least 12 hours in the refrigerator before serving with its slightly jellified sauce.

SPICED BAKED FALL FRUIT

INGREDIENTS (SERVES 6)

6 peaches

6 large plums

Butter, for greasing

2 Tbsp Kirsch or 2 Tbsp orange juice

1 tsp ground cardamom

¼ tsp ground nutmeg

½ tsp ground cinnamon

1 tsp white pepper, crushed

2 Tbsp muscovado sugar

METHOD—Preheat the oven to 400°F [200°C]. Wash the fruit, halve it, and remove the stones. Grease an ovenproof dish large enough to hold all the fruit with a little butter. Add the Kirsch or orange juice. Place the fruit skin-side down into the dish and sprinkle them evenly with the spices. Sprinkle the sugar over the top and roast in the oven about 15 minutes, or until tender, depending on the size and ripeness of the fruit. By the end of cooking you should have a syrupy sauce at the bottom of the dish. Remove from the oven and serve with rice pudding, or simply with cream.

ROQUEFORT
PEARS & WALNUTS

This simple assembly is what I like most often when I come to the end of a meal.

INGREDIENTS (SERVES 6)

1¼ cup [100 g] Roquefort cheese, or other crumbly, strong blue cheese, such as Stilton

4 ripe pears, such as Comice or Williams

½ cup [50 g] walnuts, shelled

A dribble of walnut oil

METHOD—Crumble the cheese into fork-size pieces and put in a bowl. Core and slice the pears into wedges and add to the bowl, then add the walnuts. Drizzle with walnut oil and toss gently. Divide between four plates and serve.

STICKY TOFFEE PUDDING

A totally stodgy, sticky, and sweet dessert. Perfect.

INGREDIENTS (SERVES 6)
BATTER:

7 Tbsp [100 g] butter, softened, plus extra for greasing

6½ oz [180 g] dates, stoned and chopped

1 tsp baking soda

5 Tbsp [75 g] dark muscovado sugar

5 Tbsp [75 g] superfine sugar

1 large egg, beaten

1½ cups [170 g] flour, sifted

1 tsp baking powder

½ tsp ground cinnamon

SAUCE:

7 Tbsp [100 g] unsalted butter

½ cup [100 g] brown sugar

½ cup [120 ml] heavy cream

METHOD—Preheat the oven to 350°F [180°C] and grease an 8½ in [22 cm] cake tin with butter.

Put the dates in a bowl with 1 cup [250 ml] boiling water and the baking soda. Set aside. Beat together the butter and sugars until pale and fluffy. Slowly beat in the egg, followed by the flour, baking powder, and cinnamon. Finally, add the dates and their liquid and combine well.

Pour the batter into the prepared tin and bake about 35 minutes, or until a skewer inserted into the center of the comes out dry.

Meanwhile, prepare the toffee sauce. Heat all the ingredients gently until the butter is melted, then bring to a boil. Simmer a few minutes, until the sauce is smooth, light brown, and sticks to the back of a spoon.

When the pudding is baked, preheat the grill to high. Remove the pudding from the tin, place on a heatproof serving dish, and pierce the surface a few times with a skewer. Spoon over the toffee sauce, put for a few moments under the grill until it bubbles—be careful not to burn it. Serve straightaway with cream or ice cream.

CLASSIC BLOODY MARY

A good Bloody Mary is halfway between a food and a drink with its thick consistency, meatiness, salt, and spice. Whether deployed as a straightener, pick-me-up, or enlivener, it's a classic. There are many Marys and what constitutes the "true" version is the subject of fierce debate. This classic Mary is a bare-bones version, around which you can develop your own way.

INGREDIENTS (SERVES 1)

3 Tbsp vodka
A capful of dry sherry, Fino or Manzanilla
A squeeze of lemon juice
A couple of twists of black pepper
A pinch of celery salt
   (or sea salt if unavailable)
A few good shakes of Tabasco, or to taste
   (or other chili of choice)
About 6 good shakes of Worcestershire sauce
Chilled tomato juice, to top up

METHOD—Fill a highball glass with ice. Pour over the vodka. Add all the other ingredients except the tomato juice and stir well. Top up the glass with tomato juice, stir, and serve.

BLOODY DIRTY MARY

This is a really well-spiced Mary, which is how I like it. It's "dirty" because the extra saucing makes it a little brown. Puts hairs on your chest. Make it in the same way as the Classic, but double the quantities of lemon, black pepper, celery salt, Tabasco, and Worcestershire sauces. The possible spicing variations are endless. In particular, though, this Mary is an invitation to experiment with nonstandard chili saucing. Bloody Mary was originally made with a large pinch of cayenne pepper that was "cooked" in the lemon juice. Some people macerate chilies in their sherry bottles for an extra kick. Chipotle chili sauce works well, too.

LIKE A VIRGIN MARY

Many long-term Mary fans believe that the vodka is the odd ingredient out, as it masks the flavors of the other ingredients. That said, a Virgin Mary (without any alcohol) was probably not why you wanted a cocktail in the first place! Welcome to the Like a Virgin Mary. It's like a Virgin Mary, except for the fact that it has alcohol in it.

Replace the vodka with an equal amount of dry sherry, such as Fino or Manzanilla.

PRAIRIE FIRE

INGREDIENTS (MAKES 1)
3 Tbsp white tequila (100 percent agave)
3 drops Tabasco sauce

METHOD—Pour the tequila into a shot glass. Add the Tabasco sauce. Don't stir.

MANHATTAN

One of the all-time classics. Do try to use rye whiskey rather than bourbon, which tends to be overly sweet and claggy.

INGREDIENTS (MAKES 1)
¼ cup [60 ml] rye whiskey
2 Tbsp red vermouth
2 dashes Angostura bitters
Ice cubes
1 Maraschino cherry (optional)

METHOD—Pour the rye, vermouth, and Angostura bitters in a mixing glass and add some ice. Stir 10 seconds.

Strain into a martini glass or serve on the rocks in a tumbler and add the Maraschino cherry, if using.

To make yourself a dryer, "perfect" Manhattan, replace half the red vermouth with dry vermouth. Lip smacking.

SALTY DOG

INGREDIENTS (MAKES 1)

¼ cup [60 ml] vodka

½ cup [120 ml] grapefruit juice

¼ tsp salt

5 to 6 ice cubes

METHOD—Fill a short tumbler with all the ingredients except the ice. Stir to dissolve the salt, then add 5 to 6 ice cubes, stir again, and serve.

GIMLET

INGREDIENTS (MAKES 1)

¼ cup [60 ml] gin

4 tsp lime cordial

Cracked ice

METHOD—Place the gin and lime cordial in a cocktail shaker with the ice.

Shake and strain into a martini glass.

HOT BUTTERED RUM

INGREDIENTS (MAKES 1)

1½ tsp superfine sugar

½ cup [120 ml] boiling water

1 pinch each ground cinnamon, ground clove, and
    grated nutmeg

¼ cup [60 ml] dark rum

1 tsp unsalted butter

The traditional way of heating this winter warmer is to ram a red-hot poker into the glass. Personally, I'm not so sure that red-hot pokers and alcohol mix well.

METHOD—Mix together the sugar and boiling water in a heatproof glass or mug and stir until it dissolves.

Add the spices and stir in well, then add the rum and butter. Stir and serve.

MARGARITA

This punchy mix of salt and sour distracts you from the alcohol. Never place large bets in a Mexican bar if you can no longer recollect how many of these you have drunk. Trust me.

INGREDIENTS (MAKES 1)

Fine salt, for frosting

3 Tbsp white tequila (100 percent agave)

4 tsp lime juice

2 tsp triple sec

Ice cubes

METHOD—Pour the salt onto a plate to a depth of $\frac{1}{16}$ in [2 mm]. Moisten the rim of a martini glass with water and place it upside down on the plate to frost the rim.

Place the remaining ingredients in a cocktail shaker. Shake 10 seconds, then strain into the frosted glass. Serve immediately.

ZAZA

Dubonnet on its own is not all that interesting, but it pairs beautifully with gin.

INGREDIENTS (MAKES 1)

2 Tbsp Dubonnet

3 Tbsp gin

3 drops Angostura bitters

Ice cubes

Lemon or orange peel

METHOD—Place the Dubonnet, gin, and Angostura bitters in a mixing glass with the ice and stir 10 seconds. Strain into a martini glass or tumbler, twist a piece of lemon or orange peel over it to release the essential oils, and drop it in.

VESPER (007)

"A dry martini," he said. "One. In a deep Champagne goblet."

"*Oui, monsieur.*"

"Just a moment. Three measures of Gordon's, one of vodka, half a measure of Kina Lillet. Shake it very well until it's ice cold, then add a large, thin slice of lemon peel. Got it?"

—Ian Fleming, *Casino Royale* (1953)

EXTRA-DRY VODKA MARTINI

Stirred, not shaken. Sorry, James.

INGREDIENTS (MAKES 1)

Dry vermouth, for rinsing the glass

¼ cup [60 ml] good-quality vodka

Ice cubes

1 green olive, washed and dried

METHOD—Rinse the inside of a martini glass with the vermouth and pour out the excess.

Put the vodka and ice into a tumbler and stir 10 seconds. Strain it into the martini glass, add the olive, and serve.

OLD FASHIONED

INGREDIENTS (MAKES 1)

1 sugar cube

4 drops Angostura bitters

¼ cup [60 ml] rye whiskey

2 tsp soda water

Ice cubes

1 strip orange zest

METHOD—Place a sugar cube in a tumbler and sprinkle the Angostura bitters onto the sugar. Crush with a spoon.

Add the rye and muddle together. Add the soda water and ice and stir.

Twist the zest over the glass to release the essential oils in the skin and drop it in. Serve immediately.

CORPSE REVIVER Nº2

INGREDIENTS (MAKES 1)

Absinthe, for rinsing the glass

2 Tbsp gin

2 Tbsp Cointreau

2 Tbsp Lillet blanc

2 Tbsp fresh lemon juice

Ice cubes

METHOD—Rinse a martini glass with absinthe and pour out the excess.

Place the gin, Cointreau, Lillet blanc, and lemon juice in a cocktail shaker with the ice. Shake 30 seconds, then strain into the absinthe-flavored glass. Serve immediately.

HEMINGWAY DAIQUIRI

INGREDIENTS (MAKES 1)

3 Tbsp white rum

2 tsp fresh lime juice

1 tsp grapefruit juice

1 tsp Maraschino liqueur

Crushed ice

METHOD—Shake all the ingredients in a cocktail shaker 10 seconds and strain into a martini glass. Serve immediately.

FLAMING ABSINTHE

Take a dance with the Green Fairy.

INGREDIENTS (SERVES 4)

14 Tbsp [200 ml] cold water

Ice cubes

2 tsp sugar cane syrup

4 tsp absinthe

METHOD—Mix half the water with the ice in a tumbler. In a second tumbler, combine the remaining water with the sugar cane syrup.

Pour the absinthe carefully into the glass over the convex side of a mixing spoon, so that it floats in a layer on top. Ignite with a match. Take care, as the flame can appear almost invisible. Extinguish after 3 seconds by placing a saucer on top of the glass.

Empty the tumbler with the ice water and pour the cocktail into the chilled glass. Serve immediately.

THE BASICS

CHICKEN STOCK

INGREDIENTS (MAKES 4½ CUPS [1 L])

- 1 boiling chicken, or 2¼ lb [1 kg] chicken carcasses and wings, rinsed
- 8¾ oz [250 g] carrots, diced
- 8¾ oz [250 g] celery root, diced
- 2 leeks, white part only, quartered
- 2 onions, quartered
- 1 bay leaf
- 2 cloves

METHOD—Place all the ingredients in a large casserole dish with 6½ cups [1.5 L] cold water. Bring to a boil, then reduce the heat, so the stock barely simmers. Using a slotted spoon, skim off any scum. Let it simmer gently 1½ hours.

Strain through a sieve lined with muslin. Let cool, then keep refrigerated.

BEEF STOCK

INGREDIENTS (MAKES 4½ CUPS [1 L])

- 2¼ lb [1 kg] beef bones, coarsely chopped, rinsed
- 2 large onions, halved
- A few stems fresh flat-leaf parsley and tarragon
- A few stems thyme
- 1 bay leaf
- 2 celery stalks, roughly chopped
- 2 carrots, roughly chopped
- 1 large tomato, halved
- 2 garlic cloves
- 1 star anise (optional)
- Salt and black pepper

METHOD—Preheat the oven to 425°F [220°C]. Put the beef bones and onions in a roasting tray, season well with salt and pepper, and roast in the oven 30 minutes.

Remove the bones and onions and carefully place them in a large pan, removing any blackened onion pieces first. Add 2½ qt [2.5 L] cold water to the pan and bring to a boil.

After a couple of minutes, skim off any scum that has risen to the surface with a slotted spoon. Tie the herbs together with kitchen string. Reduce the heat so that the stock barely simmers and add the rest of the ingredients. Simmer gently about 3 hours. Check that there is enough liquid, top up when necessary, and skim from time to time.

Strain out all the solids through a sieve lined with muslin. Let cool, then keep refrigerated.

CHINESE PORK & CHICKEN STOCK

INGREDIENTS (MAKES 4½ CUPS [1 L])

1 x 3 lb [1.5 kg] boiling chicken, or chicken
  carcasses and wings

1⅔ lb [750 g] pork bones with some meat attached,
  such as ribs or neck

1 bunch scallions, chopped

2 in [5 cm] fresh ginger root, chopped

Salt and black pepper

METHOD—Rinse the chicken and bones in plenty of cold water and place in a large pan. Add enough cold water to cover completely. Bring to a boil, reduce the heat, and simmer 10 minutes, skimming with a slotted spoon to remove any scum.

After 10 minutes, discard the liquid and reserve the meat and bones. Wash and scrub them thoroughly under plenty of cold water. Clean the pan to remove any scum. Return the meat and bones to the pan, add the scallions and ginger, and cover with about 6¼ qt [6 L] cold water. Do not add salt at any time during the cooking—season it at the end. Bring to a boil, reduce the heat, and simmer very gently 6 hours. Do not cover. Taste and season with salt and pepper if necessary.

Strain the stock through a sieve lined with muslin and let cool. Refrigerate for a few hours; once the stock has thoroughly chilled, remove and discard any fat on the surface with a spoon.

FISH STOCK

INGREDIENTS (MAKES 4½ CUPS [1 L])

2 Tbsp butter

2 shallots, chopped

2¼ lb [1 kg] fish heads, bones and trimmings

½ fennel bulb, diced

1 onion, diced

1 celery stalk, diced

3 oz [80 g] button mushrooms, sliced

1 bay leaf

4 white peppercorns

1 piece lemon zest

5 fresh flat-leaf parsley sprigs

1 cup [250 ml] dry white wine

1 Tbsp lemon juice

METHOD—In a large pan, melt the butter over low heat, add the shallots, and cook 3 minutes. Add the fish bones and trimmings and the remaining vegetables and heat through. Add the bay leaf, peppercorns, lemon zest, and parsley, then top up with the white wine and lemon juice.

Let the wine reduce a little before adding 4½ cups [1 L] cold water. Gently simmer 30 minutes, regularly removing any scum with a slotted spoon.

Strain through a sieve lined with muslin. Let cool, then keep refrigerated.

VEAL STOCK

INGREDIENTS (MAKES 4½ CUPS [1 L])

2¼ lb [1 kg] veal bones, coarsely chopped, rinsed

2 onions, chopped

2 celery stalks, chopped

2 carrots, chopped

2 large tomatoes, chopped

2 garlic cloves, peeled

3½ oz [100 g] mushrooms, trimmed and sliced
  (optional)

A few stems fresh flat-leaf parsley, chervil,
  and tarragon

A few stems fresh thyme

1 bay leaf

METHOD—Preheat the oven to 425°F [220°C]. Put the bones in a roasting tray and roast in the oven 20 minutes, or until brown.

Remove the bones and carefully put them in a large pan. Add 2½ qt [2.5 L] cold water to the pan and bring to a boil.

After a couple of minutes, skim off any scum that has risen to the surface using a slotted spoon. Reduce the heat so that the stock barely simmers and add the rest of the ingredients. Simmer gently about 3 hours. Check that there is enough liquid, top up when necessary, and skim from time to time.

Strain out all the solids through a sieve lined with muslin. Let cool, then keep refrigerated.

DEMI-GLACE—Make the veal stock as described above, then strain and bring back to a simmer. Cook gently until the volume has reduced by one-third.

VEGETABLE STOCK

INGREDIENTS (MAKES 4½ CUPS [1 L])

8¾ oz [250 g] carrots, finely diced

8¾ oz [250 g] celery root, finely diced

3 leeks, white part only, finely sliced

2 onions, sliced

2 garlic cloves

1 bay leaf

2 whole cloves

4 white peppercorns

1 cup [250 ml] dry white wine

METHOD—Place all the ingredients in a large casserole dish with 4½ cups [1 L] cold water. Bring to a boil. Using a slotted spoon, skim off the scum. Reduce the heat and simmer very gently 1 hour.

Strain through a sieve lined with muslin. Let cool, then keep refrigerated.

WEST INDIAN
HOT PEPPER SAUCE

INGREDIENTS (MAKES 4½ CUPS [1 L])

2¼ lb [1 kg] fresh red Scotch bonnet chilies

1 onion, finely chopped

3 garlic cloves, finely chopped

½ tsp turmeric

1½ tsp salt

3 Tbsp white wine vinegar

METHOD—Remove the stalks and seeds from the chilies—it's a good idea to wear gloves while doing this. Place all the ingredients in a saucepan and bring to a boil over high heat, stirring constantly. Cook briskly 1 minute, then remove and let cool slightly.

Pour the chili mixture into a blender and process to your preferred consistency. Let cool to room temperature, then pour into sterilized jars.

To sterilize jars, wash the jars and their lids and seals in very hot, soapy water, rinse, and put in a very low oven 10 minutes, or until completely dry. Keep them warm until you fill them. Handle them with clean dish towels or oven gloves and do not touch the insides before filling them. Seal the jars tightly after filling them.

MANGO CHUTNEY

There's no comparison between the cloying mass that most commercial chutneys consist of, and your own homemade preserve. This recipe produces a fragrant, juicy-yet-spicy chutney that will improve your cold cuts and Indian takeouts considerably.

INGREDIENTS (MAKES ABOUT 1⅔ LB [750 G])

- 4 large mangos, peeled and sliced
- 2 apples, peeled, cored, and diced
- 4 garlic cloves, crushed
- 1¼ in [3 cm] fresh ginger root, peeled and grated
- 2 cups [400 g] sugar
- 1 Tbsp mustard seeds
- 4 cloves
- 1 Tbsp chili powder
- 1 tsp salt
- 1 cinnamon stick
- 1 cup [250 ml] cider vinegar

METHOD—Combine all the ingredients except the vinegar in a large bowl and stir well. Cover and leave to macerate 8 hours.

Transfer to a casserole dish, add the vinegar, and bring to a boil over medium heat. Reduce the heat and simmer gently about 40 minutes, stirring frequently, or until thickened. Spoon into sterilized jars (see p. 251) while still hot, and seal immediately. Leave to mature for a couple of weeks before serving. Unopened, it will keep for a couple of years in a cool, dry place.

TOMATO CHUTNEY

INGREDIENTS (MAKES ABOUT 1⅛ LB [500 G])

3 lb [1.5 kg] tomatoes

5¼ oz [150 g] dried apricots, chopped

2 in [5 cm] fresh ginger root, peeled and chopped

6 garlic cloves, chopped

2½ cups [300 g] sugar

1¼ cups [300 ml] cider vinegar

1 Tbsp salt

1 Tbsp cayenne pepper

METHOD—Put the tomatoes in a heatproof bowl and pour over boiling water to cover. Leave 1 to 2 minutes, then remove them with a slotted spoon as soon as the skin cracks. Let cool slightly, then remove the skins, cut them into quarters, and discard the seeds.

Place all the ingredients in a large casserole and bring to a boil over medium heat. Reduce the heat to very low and simmer gently 2 hours, stirring frequently, until thickened. Spoon into sterilized jars (see p. 251) while still hot, and seal immediately. Leave to mature for a couple of weeks before serving. Unopened, it will keep for a couple of years in a cool, dry place.

HORSERADISH SAUCE

Have this alongside your pot roast.

INGREDIENTS (SERVES 6)

3 Tbsp grated fresh horseradish

2 tsp lemon juice

Pinch of sugar

1 cup [250 ml] whipping cream

Salt and black pepper

METHOD—Mix the horseradish with the lemon juice and sugar. Whip the cream until it just holds soft peaks, and then fold the horseradish mixture into it. Season with salt and pepper. Store in the refrigerator and use within 2 days.

TARTARE SAUCE

INGREDIENTS (SERVES 4)

2 egg yolks

1 Tbsp mustard

1½ cups [350 ml] groundnut oil

2 Tbsp lemon juice

3 cornichons, chopped

2 tsp capers, chopped

½ bunch fresh flat-leaf parsley, chopped

Salt and black pepper

METHOD—Place the egg yolks and mustard in a nonmetallic bowl and whisk them together. Still whisking continuously, slowly pour in the oil, little by little, until you obtain a thick, creamy texture like mayonnaise. Stir in the lemon juice, cornichons, capers, and parsley, and season well with salt and pepper.

KETCHUP

INGREDIENTS (MAKES 2 CUPS [500 ML])

1 bay leaf
½ tsp whole cloves
½ tsp allspice berries
1 cinnamon stick
2¼ lb [1 kg] ripe tomatoes, roughly chopped
1 onion, chopped
2 garlic cloves, crushed
4½ Tbsp [70 g] soft brown sugar
⅝ cup [150 ml] cider vinegar
1 tsp cayenne pepper
1 tsp salt
Black pepper

Heinz ketchup is great, really it is. It claims on the bottle that "no other ketchup tastes quite like it." I agree—try mine.

METHOD—Tie the spices in a small piece of clean cloth or muslin and secure with kitchen string. Combine the remaining ingredients in a large pan, bring to a boil, and simmer 45 minutes. Remove the spice bag and push the sauce through a coarse-meshed sieve back into the same pan. Return the pan to the heat, add the spice bag, and continue to cook over low heat about 20 minutes, or until thickened. Season with more salt and black pepper if needed. Spoon warm into sterilized glass bottles or jars (see p. 251) and keep in the refrigerator. Opened, it will keep for approximately 4 weeks. If sealed immediately after bottling, it will keep for a year in a cool, dry place.

CHIPOTLE IN ADOBO

This is an addictive Mexican marinade, and very versatile. Excellent as a barbecue sauce.

INGREDIENTS (MAKES ABOUT 2 QT [2 L])

PICKLED CHIPOTLE:

8¾ oz [250 g] chipotle chilies, destalked and seeded

4 garlic cloves

2 bay leaves

1 fresh thyme sprig

2 cups [500 ml] cider vinegar

ADOBO:

¼ cup [50 g] ancho chilies, destalked and seeded

2 Tbsp mulatto chilies, destalked and seeded
  (if available, otherwise replace with anchos)

1 cup [250 ml] olive oil

1 large onion, chopped

4 garlic cloves, chopped

3 carrots, peeled and sliced

2 cups [150 g] piloncillo, grated, or dark brown sugar

1⅛ lb [500 g] tomatoes, skinned and chopped

2 tsp dried oregano

2 avocado leaves (alternatively, use bay leaves)

1 tsp dried thyme

2 tsp salt

METHOD—Put the prepared chipotles in a jar together with the garlic and herbs. In a saucepan, bring the vinegar to a boil and pour over the chilies. Leave to macerate in the jar overnight, turning occasionally. The chilies will absorb the vinegar almost entirely.

When ready to prepare the adobo, bring water to a boil and soak the ancho and mulatto chilies, off the heat, 15 minutes. Purée the chilies with 1½ cups [350 ml] of the soaking liquid. Set aside. Drain the chipotle chilies and remove the herbs and garlic.

Heat the olive oil in a skillet over low heat and add the chopped onion. Soften 5 minutes before adding the garlic and carrots. Cook 10 minutes over low heat and add the sugar. Increase the heat to medium. Stir to dissolve the sugar. After a few minutes, add the tomatoes, herbs, salt, and the puréed ancho and mulatto chilies. Cook 10 minutes and add the pickled chipotle chilies. Bring to a boil, reduce the heat, and simmer a further 10 minutes. Pour into sterilized jars and seal while still hot (see p. 251). Leave to macerate for at least 2 weeks before opening. They should keep in a cool, dry place for several months.

SALSA VERDE

INGREDIENTS (SERVES 6)

3½ oz [100 g] fresh flat-leaf parsley, leaves chopped

2 garlic cloves, finely chopped

4 anchovies, finely chopped

2½ Tbsp capers, roughly chopped

2 Tbsp fine white breadcrumbs (optional)

1 to 2 Tbsp lemon juice

7 Tbsp [100 ml] good-quality olive oil

METHOD—Mix the parsley with the garlic, anchovies, and capers in a bowl. Add the breadcrumbs, if using. Next, add the lemon juice and slowly pour in the oil, stirring constantly—you need just enough for a loose, but not runny, consistency. If you prefer a slightly thickened consistency, add the breadcrumbs. Store in the refrigerator, where it will keep for a couple of days.

HARISSA

INGREDIENTS (MAKES ABOUT 14 OZ [400 G])

8¾ oz [250 g] dried hot chilies

1 Tbsp caraway seeds

6 garlic cloves, chopped

1 Tbsp ground coriander

2 tsp salt

1 Tbsp lemon juice

Olive oil, for processing

This is the ubiquitous hot sauce of North Africa. Although ready-made is acceptable, this homemade version is quick, easy, and (call me biased), better.

METHOD—Soak the chilies in hot water 1 hour. Drain, then remove the stalks and seeds. Roughly chop them. Lightly toast the caraway seeds in a dry skillet over medium heat until fragrant, then tip them out immediately.

Place all the ingredients in a blender. Process, adding a drizzle of olive oil to make a smooth paste. Add a little water if the paste is too thick. Pour into small sterilized jars (see p. 251) and pour a layer of olive oil on top. It will keep refrigerated for several weeks.

SALAD DRESSING № 1

Why anyone would bother to buy a ready-made dressing is beyond me. You can fix up a dressing in less than 3 minutes, and it's usually vastly superior in flavor. Here's a classic French mustard dressing and a blue cheese version. You be the judge.

INGREDIENTS (SERVES 4 to 6)

1 garlic clove
1 tsp Dijon mustard
1 tsp honey
2 Tbsp white wine vinegar
2 Tbsp olive oil
4 Tbsp grapeseed oil (or other neutral-flavored oil)
Coarse salt and black pepper

METHOD—Roughly chop the garlic and put it on a chopping board with a little coarse salt; using the whole blade of the knife, press and work it into a smooth paste.

Put the crushed garlic in a bowl with the mustard and honey, and season with salt and pepper. Add the vinegar and stir it in until dissolved. Gradually add both types of oil, whisking continuously, until emulsified.

SALAD DRESSING № 2

INGREDIENTS (SERVES 4 to 6)

1 garlic clove
¾ cup [60 g] blue cheese, crumbled
1 Tbsp white wine vinegar
1 Tbsp lemon juice
4 Tbsp groundnut oil
Salt and black pepper

METHOD—Roughly chop the garlic and put it on a chopping board with a little coarse salt; using the whole blade of the knife, press and work it into a smooth paste.

Put the crushed garlic in a bowl and stir in the blue cheese. Add a couple of grinds of pepper, the vinegar, and lemon juice. Stir, then add the oil, whisking continuously until it emulsifies.

FLAT BREAD

INGREDIENTS (MAKES 10)

2 cups [250 g] strong white bread flour, sifted

2 cups [250 g] wholemeal bread flour, sifted

2 tsp dried fast-action yeast

½ tsp sugar

2 tsp salt

2 Tbsp olive oil, plus extra for greasing

METHOD—Combine the flours, yeast, sugar, and salt in a bowl. Add 1¼ cups [300 ml] water and the oil and combine to make a dough, adding a little more water if necessary. Knead 10 minutes, until smooth and pliable. Transfer to a lightly greased bowl, cover with plastic wrap, and leave to rise in a warm place 1 to 2 hours, or until doubled in size.

Put on the work surface, punch the air out, and divide into 10 pieces. Using a rolling pin, roll each piece into an oval shape about 6 in [16 cm] long, then cover and leave to rest 30 minutes in a warm place.

Preheat the grill to its highest setting. Heat a heavy-based skillet, without any oil, over a high heat. Once the pan is very hot, add the first batch of breads to the pan and fry on one side until the dough puffs up and the bottom gets slightly charred—about 1 minute. Remove and put under the hot grill, with the uncooked side facing up, until slightly charred (about 3 to 4 minutes). Brush with a little olive oil, and serve.

NAAN BREAD

INGREDIENTS (MAKES 8)

1½ tsp dried yeast

1 tsp sugar

3¼ cups [400 g] flour, plus extra for dusting

1 tsp salt

3 Tbsp clarified butter, melted, plus extra for frying, greasing, and brushing

½ cup [100 ml] yogurt

Flavorless oil, if needed

METHOD—Combine the dried yeast with ¾ cup [170 ml] warm water and the sugar, stir well, and set aside 10 minutes, until it is foamy. Sieve the flour into a mixing bowl and add the salt. Add the yeast mixture, melted butter, and yogurt and combine to a smooth dough. If the mixture is too sticky, add a few drops of oil. If it is too dry, add a little more water.

Knead 10 minutes, until smooth and supple, cover with lightly greased plastic wrap, and leave in a warm place at least 1 hour, or until doubled in volume. Knead it again 10 minutes.

Preheat the grill to its highest setting. Dust a clean work surface with flour. Divide the dough into 8 pieces and roll each one out to an oval shape. Stretch them a little with your hands. Heat a skillet over high heat and add a little butter. Fry the naan breads on one side only 2 minutes, then transfer onto a baking sheet with the uncooked side facing up. Brush with clarified butter and cook under the grill 2 minutes, or until lightly charred.

TORTILLAS

It is quite satisfying to make your own tortillas. The key ingredient is *masa harina*, a Mexican corn flour. If your local store does not offer it, order it online, as it makes a vast difference in taste and texture compared to using wheat flour.

INGREDIENTS (SERVES 12)

8¾ oz [250 g] masa harina

½ tsp salt

3 Tbsp cold lard (alternatively, use oil or butter)

METHOD—Combine the masa harina and salt in a bowl and add the cold lard. Rub it between your fingers until you have a crumbly mixture. Slowly add 1¼ cups [300 ml] warm water, bring together, and knead a few minutes to achieve a soft dough. Add more liquid if the dough is too dry, or a little more flour if too wet. Cover with plastic wrap and leave to rest 30 minutes.

Divide the dough into 12 parts and shape them into rounds the size of a golf ball. Cover these with a damp cloth while you prepare each tortilla.

Put a sheet of plastic wrap on the work surface, add a piece of dough, and put another sheet of plastic wrap on top. Using a heavy pot or large plate, press out the dough until it is about 1/16 in [2 mm] thin and 5 in [13 cm] diameter.

Put a heavy-based skillet over medium heat. Once it is hot, carefully remove the plastic wrap sheets from the tortilla and put swiftly into the hot pan. Cook 1 minute on each side, then remove and wrap in paper towels to keep warm while you cook the others.

BURGER BUNS

INGREDIENTS (MAKES 10)
DOUGH:

4 cups [500 g] strong white bread flour, sifted,
  plus extra for dusting

4 tsp dried fast-action yeast

2 tsp salt

4 tsp sugar

2 Tbsp butter, melted and slightly cooled,
  plus extra for greasing

1 egg, lightly beaten

GLAZE:

1 egg white

10 tsp sesame seeds

METHOD—Combine the flour, yeast, salt, and sugar in a bowl. Add the melted, slightly cooled butter, egg, and 14 Tbsp [200 ml] warm water, and combine to make a dough. Add a little more water if necessary. Knead on a lightly floured surface about 10 minutes, until you have a soft, silky dough. Return the dough to the mixing bowl and cover with a dish towel. Leave to rise in a warm place until doubled in volume—about 1 to 2 hours.

Line a baking sheet with baking parchment. Divide the dough into 10 pieces, roll them into balls, and shape them into buns by slightly flattening them. Put them on the baking sheet. Cover with lightly greased plastic wrap and leave to rise until they have noticeably puffed up—about 1 hour.

Preheat the oven to 350°F [180°C]. Brush the buns with the egg white and sprinkle the sesame seeds on top. Bake 17 to 20 minutes, or until golden. Remove from the oven and let cool on a wire rack.

THE FUNDAMENT

On one level, barbecuing is the most basic of all cookery, and has changed little since we lived in caves: it's primal, and that's part of the fun. But we have learned some tricks along the way, and they can make all the difference.

Where I am still very much in agreement with our ancient ancestors is that we need not worry too much about which type of barbecue we have. An adjustable rack that allows you to get very close or very far from the coals is the most important feature of any barbecue. A lid really helps, especially if you want to smoke things, but you can live without it. A large area on which to cook different ingredients is desirable, but won't make your cooking any better. Clever, newfangled things like thermometers are merely nice additions.

Got a gas barbecue? Boot her up, press go, or whatever it is you do. Charcoal? Now, that's a different matter. To start a charcoal fire, put a few firelighter cubes at the base of your barbecue and arrange a couple of handfuls of kindling wood in a wigwam shape around them, leaving a little opening, just like a real wigwam. Light the firelighters and wait for the fire to take hold on the kindling. Now start to make a small pile of charcoal all around and on top of your flaming wigwam, using tongs.

AVOID ROOKIE ERROR #1:
FAILING TO LIGHT THE BARBECUE.
Work fast but carefully—you don't want to snuff out your nascent fire with an avalanche of charcoal or charcoal dust. Add the rest of your coals gradually, building a hill. Don't pour on the charcoal dust that frequently forms at the bottom of the bag. Rescue the coals that have fallen to the sides by placing them on top of your heap. The method is similar if you are using wood, but it may take longer and require more fuel to get to this point. Wood has a more subtle flavor than charcoal.

AVOID ROOKIE ERROR #2:
COOKING BEFORE THE COALS ARE READY.
Only when the flames have died down, and all the coals in the pile are glowing orange and have a covering of gray-white ash, should you spread them around the floor of the grill. Then you can begin cooking. Charcoals that are not ready will spoil the taste of your food, and the flames will utterly ruin it.

AVOID ROOKIE ERROR #3:
BARBECUE CUT SHORT DUE TO LACK OF HOT COALS.
The most disappointing barbecue is the one at which you end up cooking half the food in the oven because the fire went out too soon. A bag with 100 or so briquettes will provide coverage for a standard small barbecue and will last for around 45 minutes of actual cooking time. If in doubt, avoid disappointment and start another barbecue or barbecue kettle about 30 to 40 minutes after you start the first one. That way you can replenish the cooking coals and cook meat safely. The second barbecue does not have to be fancy or have a functional grill, lid, or anything. Use that broken-down old thing in the yard that you never threw out. Transfer the coals carefully with a small shovel.

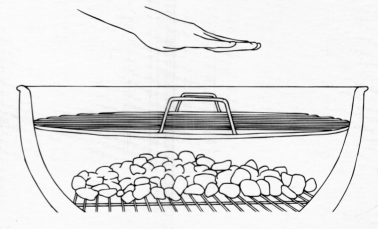

AVOID ROOKIE ERROR #4:
TRYING TO COOK EVERYTHING OVER THE SAME
HEAT IN THE SAME WAY.

You wouldn't roast a turkey and a fish in an oven in the same way at the same temperature, and it's the same for a barbecue. Understand and control the level and type of heat, and your barbecue will be transformed.

Judge your heat level. At a safe distance above the barbecue grill (about 5 in [12 cm]), extend the palm of your hand over the coals.

Count the seconds until you have to pull your hand away. Don't burn your hand.

2 to 3 seconds is high heat (450 to 575°F [230 to 300°C]).

4 to 6 seconds is medium heat (350 to 450°F [180 to 230°C]).

7 to 10 seconds is low heat (275 to 300°F [130 to 150°C]).

Make heat zones. You want to be able to cook at different temperatures over the same grill, and to cook for long periods without burning the food. To achieve both, you need to position the coals so that there is one area of direct heat and one of indirect heat. You can simply put all the coals at one side of the grate and none at the other, or alternatively you can make a space between the coals where there are none.

GRILLING BASICS

The Way of the Grill is a pleasurable lifelong pursuit. However, there are a number of simple tips that will get you a long way down the road quite quickly.

BE PREPARED
Give yourself plenty of time to prepare your barbecue and food, especially if you are marinating anything. Do all your prep work in advance.

LET THE GRILL DO ITS WORK
Turn the meat and fish only once, or just a very few times. You need to give it time to char and crisp. Be patient; moving the food around a lot stops the grill from having the desired effect.

AVOID STICKING
When your food sticks to the grill you lose some of the charring you worked so hard to achieve. Torn food will drip, leading to flare-ups and dryness. It doesn't look great, either, and you leave bits behind that need

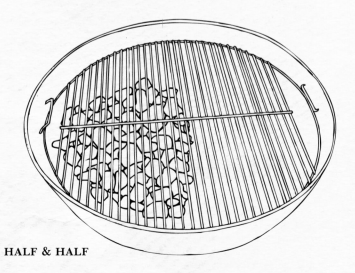

HALF & HALF

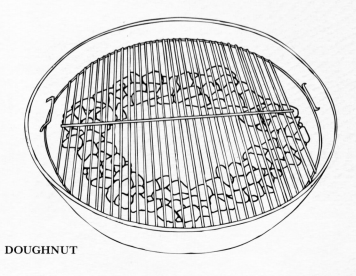

DOUGHNUT

cleaning off. To avoid sticking:

- Clean your grill properly before use.
- Without overcooking it, let the food form a crust (it will release itself in most cases).
- With fish, don't turn it more than once, as every time you turn the fish you're creating a new opportunity for the skin to stick and tear.

AVOID FLARE-UPS

Flare-ups are caused when oil and other liquids hit the coals, and you don't want that—the flames will burn your food and give it a nasty flavor. There will always be a little bit of a flare-up, though, and when this happens, just move your food out of the flames. To minimize their frequency:

- Only cook when the flames have died down.
- Trim any unwanted fat off your meat.
- Oil the food, and not the grill.
- Don't baste with oil or excessive amounts of oily or sugary marinades over the open grill.

MASTER THE FIRE

News flash: foods cook differently at different temperatures. Master the basics.

- High, direct heats and a short cooking time are best for cooking thin cuts of meat and fish, or those that require a good amount of charring before being moved to a cooler part of the grill to finish cooking.
- Fish, chicken, and vegetables are usually best cooked over medium heat.
- Low, indirect heat and long cooking times are best for ribs, whole chickens, and joints.

TEST FOR DONENESS

There are a few foods for which rareness is a desirable state of affairs: a good steak or beef burger or a fresh tuna steak, for example. But rare is not raw, and

undercooking chicken and pork can be dangerous. Always make sure your meat is properly cooked. Use a digital thermometer to check that your meat and poultry has reached the minimum internal temperature (145°F [65°C] for lamb, 160°F [70°C] for burgers, 160°F [70°C] for roasts, 165°F [75°C] for poultry). Check that the juices run clear by inserting a sharp knife or skewer in the thickest part; if you're unsure, make an incision and look at the flesh. At this point, forget about presentation and the potential loss of juices: better to be safe than sorry.

Judging the doneness of a steak takes practice and steaks pass from rare to quite well-done fairly quickly. Practice makes perfect, but you can use this well-worn touch test, too.

RARE

MEDIUM-RARE

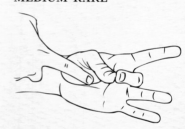

MEDIUM

WELL DONE

BUTCHERY GUIDE

A short guide to the techniques required to butcher and prepare your own meat for the recipes herein.

HOW TO JOINT A CHICKEN

First, remove the wishbone. Lay the chicken on its back and run your finger around the neck cavity until you feel the V-shaped wishbone. Using a sharp knife, scrape

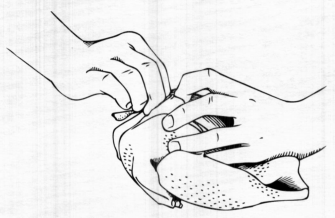

away the flesh to completely expose it. Run your knife behind the bone, now use your fingers to twist and lift the bone free.

Using a small sharp knife, cut down through the skin between the leg and carcass. Bend the leg back away from the carcass until the leg bone pops free. Cut the leg away from the backbone and repeat with the other leg.

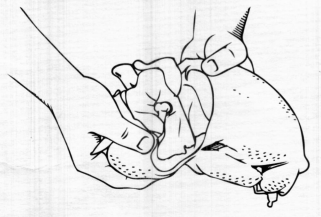

Using poultry shears, cut out the backbone, leaving just the breasts and wings. Now use the shears to cut along the breast bone from neck to tail. You now have a chicken cut into four portions.

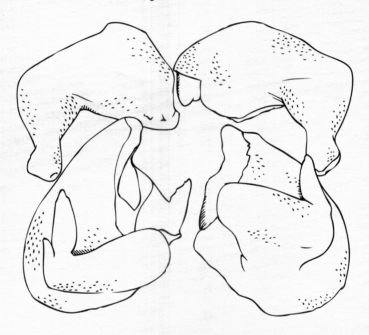

To joint a chicken into eight pieces, use the shears to cut the breasts about one third of the way down from the wings. Now divide the legs into drumstick and thigh. Find the joint with your fingers, then, using a small sharp knife, slice through it.

To joint a chicken into ten pieces, take the larger breast pieces and cut each one in two. When jointing a bird into ten, you may choose to make the initial cut separating breast and breast-and-wing piece slightly farther up the breast (three-quarters of the way up), so that there is less meat attached to the wing piece than before, leaving more to be divided between the final two joints.

HOW TO PLUCK AND GUT A PHEASANT

For wet plucking, heat a large pan of water to 140°F [60°C]. Pluck the long tail feathers out of the bird, and, holding on to the feet, plunge it into the water for 2 minutes.

Immediately start removing the feathers; the bird should be warm while you are working. Begin carefully with the neck and breasts, before removing the feathers on the thighs, wings, back, and tail. Finally, singe the bird with a long, lit match to remove the down.

To remove the feet, make an incision in the skin around the leg joints and move the legs around to loosen the cartilage. Snap the joint.

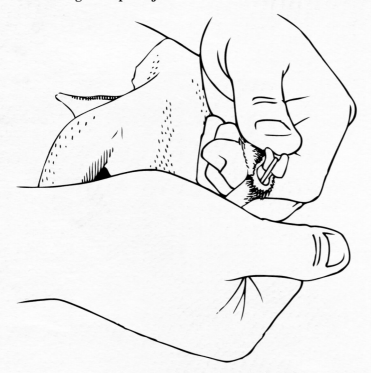

Now, holding on to the thigh tightly, pull the foot away firmly. The tendons should come off with it.

To remove the guts, cut into the lower neck just above the breast and remove the air tube and gullet with the goiter (a small gland). Cut off the head and neck.

Now put the pheasant on its back and make an incision from the anus to the base of the breast bone.

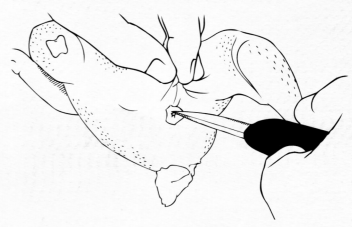

Don't cut too deeply into the bird, so that you leave the digestive tract intact—⅜ in [1 cm] is enough. Put a finger in the cavity and pull the giblets out. Remove the anal gland.

Finally, clean the pheasant by rubbing it with paper towels.

HOW TO BONE A PIG'S TROTTER

This is not difficult, but you need patience and a sharp boning knife—that is, a knife with a short, narrow blade. If you are preparing the Stuffed Pig's Trotter, you should be especially careful not to puncture the skin with the knife. Note that you need the longer, rear trotters.

Put your trotter on a board so that the underside of the foot is facing up. Make an incision lengthwise through the middle of the trotter from the hock, cleanly cutting through the skin. Working from the leg end, stretch the skin away from the bone and flesh, using your knife to cut carefully through the connective tissue and free the skin.

Now, flex the foot so that you can locate the knuckle joints. There are two. Start with the lower joint and make an incision with the knife between the ball and socket on both sides of the foot. Because of the curve in the joint, you will have to find the right angle. It becomes easier when you have started cutting. Cut away as much as you can. Then move onto the second joint, which is about half an inch or so farther up. Repeat the operation, cutting away and separating the toes and skin from the flesh and bones.

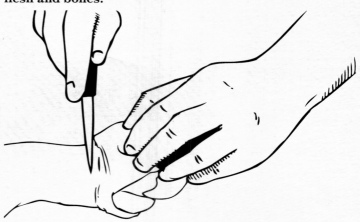

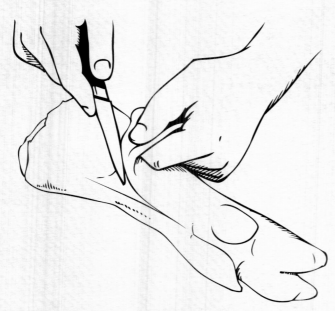

When you have two large flaps of skin, turn the trotter over and hold them both up and together and slice through any final connective tissue between them.

Take the foot and the bones in separate hands and twist a few times. You may need to make one final snip of the cord that runs through the middle of the trotter, but they should now come away easily.

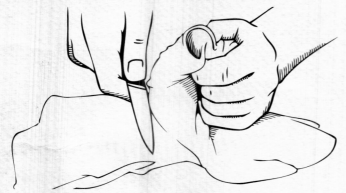

HOW TO PREPARE AND CARVE A RIB OF BEEF

When you buy your beef, ensure that the butcher has cut through the chine (back) bone so that it can be removed easily after roasting.

Before roasting a rib of beef, larder-trim the ribs. That is, expose the part-rib bones by trimming off the fat and meat along the top 2¾ in [7 cm] of the bones by cutting and scraping it away with a sharp knife. To ensure that the meat holds together during roasting, you should tie it with kitchen, or butcher's, string. Tie a piece of string around the meat between each of the rib bones and secure each one with a simple knot. The meat should be tightly trussed, without cutting into the meat.

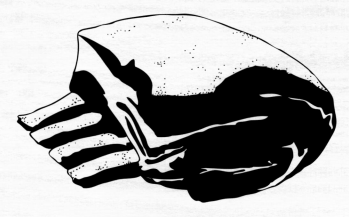

After roasting, transfer your meat to a carving board with the rib bones standing upward, and loosely cover it with foil. It is very important to rest the beef 15 to 30 minutes.

After resting, remove the string, steady the meat with a carving fork, and use a sharp carving knife to cut away the entire set of rib bones and chine bone. Discard the bones.

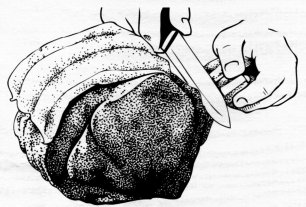

To carve, sit the meat squarely on the carving board, fat-side up, steadying with your carving fork. Cut downward across the grain, carving slices of the desired thickness using a sawing action. Let your knife do the work. A blunt knife will squeeze the juices out rather than cutting cleanly. It is also more likely to slip and cause you injury. Use a sharp knife.

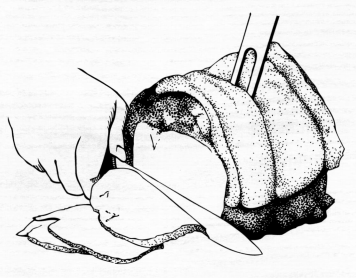

HOW TO SKIN, GUT, AND JOINT A RABBIT

Put the rabbit on a heavy chopping board or block of wood and use a meat cleaver to chop off all the feet just above the knees. Still using the cleaver, cut off the tail and remove the head.

Turn the rabbit over so that it is on its back. Lift the fur at the bottom of the belly (farthest away from the neck), make a small horizontal incision and pull the skin away from the rabbit. Insert the knife into the cut, taking care not to pierce the stomach; then, holding the knife upside down so the sharp edge faces upward, slowly and carefully cut the skin from the belly up to the neck.

Gradually pull the skin away from the rabbit's flesh. If fresh, it should come away easily. Work your way around the body of the rabbit to begin with, then upward to the front legs. The legs must be popped out through the skin. The best way to do this is to pull out the skin around the leg and push on the stump of the rabbit's leg from the other side—a bit like taking off a jacket.

Now grip the shoulders of the rabbit and pull the skin down over the back legs; again, a bit like removing an item of clothing.

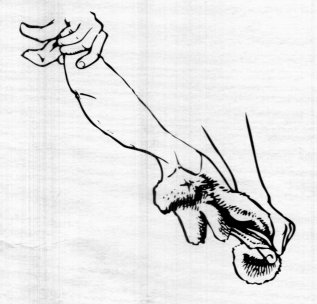

Next, gut the rabbit. Make another horizontal cut across the belly (this time trying not to pierce the intestines), and gradually slice open the stomach. Reach in and upward toward the ribs, grasp the intestines, and remove with one firm tug.

Cut through the diaphragm and pull out the lungs and heart. With a sharp knife, cut out the rabbit's tail end, make two cuts to form a V-shape where the tail was, and remove any remaining droppings from the rectum. Give the rabbit a scrub under running water and pat it dry with a clean cloth.

A rabbit is usually jointed into five sections: the two hind legs, the saddle, the two front legs, and rib cage.

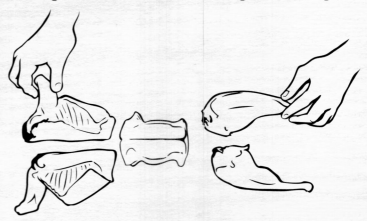

Using your cleaver, make the first chop just above the hind legs. Once separated, chop down the middle of the hind legs. Now chop the top of the saddle, just below the ribcage, then split the front legs from the torso down the spleen.

GLOSSARY

00 FLOUR
An Italian wheat flour, graded according to the 0 rating, which refers to the level of softness and how much of the wheat germ has been removed. 00 is very soft in texture and has a lower gluten content than most types of flour. There are two types: one marked *panifiable*, which is suitable for bread-making and produces a very crispy crust; the other is suitable for pasta, golden in color, and is ideal for pastry making, creating a very soft texture. If unavailable, replace with strong white bread flour for pizza dough, and all-purpose flour for pasta and pastry.

AJI AMARILLO
A type of chili used in classic Peruvian cuisine, also known as amarillo chili. Its color ranges from yellow to deep orange and the flavor is hot and slightly fruity.

AJI PANCA
Another type of chili used in classic Peruvian cuisine, which is dark red and has a smoky, fruity flavor. Both are sold dried or in paste form.

AJWAIN SEEDS
Also known as bishop's weed, carom, or ajowan, ajwain is a spice commonly used in India and Pakistan. It has a distinctive flavor of thyme with an underlying bitterness. It can easily dominate and should therefore be used sparingly.

ANCHO CHILI
Dried poblano pepper, a staple in Mexican stews and salsas. It is a mild, sweet chili with a hint of tobacco flavor. As with most dried chilies, it is usually soaked in boiled water 15 minutes before using.

ANGOSTURA BITTERS
A mixture of concentrated alcoholic bitters and water, containing gentian root and often bitter orange, whole clove, cardamom, or cinnamon, used sparingly as a flavoring for cocktails, for sauces, or desserts. It does not contain angostura bark, however.

BOUQUET GARNI
A bundle of fresh or dried herbs to flavor stocks and stews. Common components are bay leaf, parsley, thyme, and tarragon, but other herbs or spices are often added, and sometimes a stick of celery or carrot too. It is usually tied together with string, but is also sometimes wrapped and tied into a layer of leek or a piece of muslin, so that it can be removed easily at the end of cooking.

CALASPARRA RICE
A short, round-grain rice from the Calasparra region in southeast Spain. It is highly absorbent and is therefore ideally suited to dishes like paella, in which several ingredients are cooked together and the rice acquires the flavor of the cooking juices.

CASCABEL CHILI
A medium-hot chili with a nutty flavor, which is commonly cultivated in Mexico. Also known as the rattle chili, due to the loose, rattling seeds inside it when dried. It gives a beautiful deep-red color to stews and salsas.

CHIPOTLE CHILI
A hot chili popular in Mexico and Texas, with a rich, smoky, tobacco-like flavor. They are actually ripened jalapeño chilies that have been dried and smoked. In Mexican cuisine, they are often pickled, used in marinades for meat or added to stews, soups, and moles.

CLARIFIED BUTTER
Butter from which the milk solids and liquids have been removed. The pure butter fat can be heated to a much higher temperature and does not run the risk of burning. It is ideal for pan-frying and is a vital ingredient in sauces such as hollandaise. In Indian cuisine, clarified butter is known as ghee.

COTECHINO
A fresh Italian pork sausage containing a mixture of pork rind, fat, and meat from the neck and head in a natural casing. It is only lightly preserved and needs to be slow-cooked for several hours before consumption.

DRIED SHRIMP
Sun-dried shrimp used for seasoning in Chinese and South-East Asian cuisine. They have an intense aroma and are often added whole to stir-fries, crumbled in for extra seasoning, or ground for inclusion in curry pastes.

FERMENTED BLACK BEANS
Known as *douchi*, these are a Chinese specialty made from soy beans. The soy beans are fermented and then preserved in salt. The result is a black, soft, dry bean with a strong smell and a pungent, bittersweet taste.

GALANGAL
The root of the *Alpinia galangal* plant, which is used as a flavoring and is a ubiquitous ingredient in Thai cuisine. Grated, it is added to curry pastes, or it can be sliced and added to soups. Although part of the ginger family, the flavor is only faintly reminiscent of ginger. It is pungent and hot and bitter notes dominate.

GARAM MASALA
An Indian spice blend of varying composition. Common ingredients are cumin, peppercorns, cinnamon, and cardamom, among others. The spices are usually lightly toasted before being ground to a fine powder. It is often used along with other seasonings.

GREMOLATA
A mixture of chopped fresh herbs (usually flat-leaf parsley), grated lemon zest, and chopped garlic originating in Lombardy, Italy. It is added to hearty stews and roasts (particularly to osso buco) at the end of cooking, adding a fresh and fragrant counterbalance to the richness.

KEFALOTYRI
A Greek and Cypriot type of hard, salty cheese with a mildly sweet aroma. It is made of either sheep's or goat's milk, or both. Since it does not melt quickly, it is ideal in grilled and baked dishes.

LILLET BLANC
A French apéritif wine, blended from Bordeaux white wines and citrus fruit liqueurs, with a slight honey and orange flavor. It is also used as an ingredient in cocktails. Served chilled when drunk on its own.

MARASCHINO
A clear, dry liqueur made from the Marasca cherry, a variety cultivated in Croatia and northeast Italy. The stones are also used in the production, adding a bitter almond aroma. The maraschino cherry is a candied and sometimes bleached cherry that is preserved in sugar syrup and often used in cocktails. The name derives from Marasca cherries, although not all maraschino cherries are now made from that variety.

MARSALA
A Sicilian aromatic wine with an alcohol content of 15 to 20 percent. It is available in dry (*secco*), half-dry, and sweet (*dolce*) varieties. Depending on the type, it is served chilled as an apéritif or at room temperature as a dessert wine. The latter is used in cooking to flavor meat, or in desserts.

MASA HARINA
A finely ground maize flour. It is the main ingredient for making soft corn tortillas.

MULATO CHILI
A dried, mild chili with a sweet and full flavor and a chocolate note. Used in Mexican moles or salsas.

ORZO
A type of small Italian pasta with the appearance of a large rice grain. Its name means little barley. Similar pasta is found in Greek (*kritharáki*) and Turkish (*arpa şehriye*) cuisines. It is often used in soups and casseroles or as a side dish.

PASSATA

Strained tomato pulp made from puréed and sieved ripe tomatoes, the peel and seeds thereby having been removed. Passata is often used on pizza or as the basis of tomato sauce.

POMEGRANATE MOLASSES

A thick, dark, fragrant syrup made from concentrated pomegranate juice, with a sweet and tart flavor. It is used in Middle Eastern cuisine in salad dressings and marinades, as well as in cordials.

PRAGUE POWDER

A mixture of salt and sodium nitrite, which is used for curing meat. It preserves the meat, prevents the growth of bacteria, and helps preserve the color. It is colored pink to distinguish it from ordinary salt. There are two types; #1 is used for brining, and #2, which also includes sodium nitrate, is used for dry-curing.

RAS EL HANOUT

A Moroccan spice mixture that can contain many different components. A good one will contain at least 25 spices to cover a nuanced array of hot, sweet, and bitter taste notes. Common ingredients include rose petals, mace, ginger, cinnamon, nutmeg, turmeric, cloves, cardamom, and black pepper.

SHICHIMI

A Japanese spice mixture containing seven ingredients: red chili pepper, Sichuan pepper (sancho), roasted orange peel, white and black sesame seeds, ginger, hemp seeds, and nori seaweed. It is often used to flavor soups and noodles.

SICHUAN PEPPER

Not actually a type of pepper, but the dried berries of the prickly ash tree, which has a lemony and peppery aroma. Usually, only the husks are used. These have a strong mouth-numbing effect (caused by its hydroxy-alpha sanshool content). They are commonly used in Sichuanese cuisine. It is also a component of Chinese five-spice powder.

SPÄTZLE

A soft egg noodle traditionally used in southwest German cuisine. The name means "little sparrow" in Swabian dialect. The ingredients are flour, eggs, salt, and sometimes water. The dough is scraped off a wooden board directly into the boiling water. They are served either as a side dish with meats or stews, or on their own with cheese and fried onions.

ZAMPONE

An Italian sausage, which literally means "big foot," and comes from the Emilia Romagna region. It is a pig's trotter stuffed with pig's meat, which has been carefully dried for preservation. To use, the sausage has to be soaked and then cooked for several hours. Precooked versions are widely available in Italy.

INDEX

Page references in **bold** are to illustrations.

This book is dedicated to Dean Clark, crack cook, fine friend, a generous, warm, and kind man. I miss you.

ACKNOWLEDGMENTS

I would like to thank all those who took part in the making of this book: my wife Nele for her "manly" massive input, ideas, and good sense without which this book would not have happened; to Beth Evans for her incredible and inspired photography; to Anne Furniss, Helen Lewis, Laura Gladwin, and Sam Chelton for their patience, professionalism, and warm support. My apologies to my daughters, Esther and Rahel, for ignoring them shamefully while writing this book.

I would also like to thank all those who provided recipes, advice, kitchens, gardens, cooking, testing, styling, and moral support: my parents Colin and Liz Cave, Damon and Sara Summersgill, Jayne Cross, Jacques Dejonckheere, Tina Viljoen, Roman Wiech, Lindsay Walne, Erin Moroney, Nini Lane, Jan Spielhoff, Dominic and Annie Perrem, Marie-Christine Torre, Kazunori Nishibiro, Jill Mead, Domenico Buonocore, Oscar Toma, and Luca Sacco.

First published in 2013 by
Quadrille Publishing Limited,
Pentagon House,
52 to 54 Southwark Street,
London SE1 1UN
www.quadrille.com

Quadrille is an imprint of Hardie Grant
www.hardiegrant.com.au

This book was produced and designed by
Perrem & Cave
5 Crescent Row
London EC1Y 0SP

Editor: Laura Gladwin
Assistant Editor: Louise McKeever
Designer: Sam Chelton
Photography: Beth Evans
Production Director: Vincent Smith
Production Controller: James Finan

Text © 2013 Simon Cave & Nele Brauner-Cave
Photography © 2013 Beth Evans

Cataloguing in Publication Data: a catalogue record for
this book is available from the British Library.

978 184949 731 2

Printed in China